Project Management Terms

A WORKING GLOSSARY

Project Management Terms

A WORKING GLOSSARY

J. LeRoy Ward

Published by

ESI International
4301 Fairfax Drive, Suite 800
Arlington, Virginia 22203

© 2000 by ESI International

First Edition 1997
Reprinted February 1999

Printed in the United States of America

ISBN 1-890367-25-7

Contents

Preface

At ESI International, we have witnessed an incredible worldwide surge of interest in applying project management practices in a broad spectrum of industries. You need only look at the membership growth of the world's preeminent project management professional association, the Project Management Institute (PMI®), to confirm these observations. Accordingly, project management professionals must use a common and agreed-upon language to communicate not only among themselves, but with their internal sponsors and their clients, both of whom should also have at least a rudimentary knowledge of the vocabulary.

Thus, it became obvious to me that what was lacking in the field of project management, which is now widely recognized as a formal discipline, was a singular compilation of the terms that define it. So we set out to accomplish the difficult task of identifying, compiling, and defining the relevant terms and phrases. The result is this work—*Project Management Terms: A Working Glossary*.

The first edition contained more than 1,600 project management terms. Many of them are unique to the field itself (for example, budgeted cost of work performed), and some have been borrowed from other disciplines and given new meaning in the context of project management. We included most of the terms used in PMI®'s *A Guide to the Project Management Body of Knowledge* (PMBOK®). For the other 1,300 entries, we relied on the expertise of many knowledgeable professionals in the field—including my colleagues at ESI International, our clients, and the many independent consultants with whom we have worked through the years—to identify and help define the terms. As a result, this glossary represents the thoughtful, yet pragmatic, contributions of practitioners like yourself, who understand the intricacies of the business.

PMI® is a registered service mark of the Project Management Institute.
PMBOK® is a registered service mark of the Project Management Institute.

The second edition contains almost 300 new words, and we include them because project management as a discipline is not the immutable entity some would suggest. As the world ventures into such areas as e-business, m-commerce, and project management portals, our lexicon must keep pace. And, these days, the IT and product development industries are leading the way in creating our need to add to our ever-growing list of terms.

We also changed the look and size of the book to make it easier to read and to keep pace with contemporary graphic design. Its bold colors and graphic appeal are sure to attract those who would never think of picking up and reading a project management dictionary! If nothing else, the new look will enable you to find this handy work more easily on the shelves of your personal project management library.

I hope you find it a useful, valuable work.

Reston, Virginia
November 2000

About the Author

J. LeRoy Ward, a Project Management Professional (PMP®) with 26 years of experience in project management, is Senior Vice President of Global Programs for ESI International with responsibility for curriculum development and training worldwide. A PMP® since 1990, Mr. Ward has taught project management programs on five continents to people from more than 50 countries. He holds B.S. and M.S. degrees from Southern Connecticut State University and an M.S.T.M. degree, with distinction, in computer systems management from The American University. A member of several professional associations, Mr. Ward also serves on the advisory board for the Program on Project Management at The George Washington University and the editorial board of PMI®'s *PMNetwork* magazine.

About ESI International

ESI International, a wholly owned subsidiary of the International Institute of Research, is a training and consulting firm founded as Educational Services Institute in 1981. For 21 years, we have helped professionals acquire knowledge and competencies in contract management, nonprofit and public administration management, global business management, and project management.

Our one-of-a-kind curriculum has become the world's premier professional development program in project management. Professionals from around the world have benefited from seven core courses and dozens of electives leading to Master's Certificates in either Project Management or Information Technology Project Management from The George Washington University. At the end of 2000 we will have presented in just one year more than 5,200 sessions to 100,000 attendees on six continents. We also develop and teach tailored sessions for

---

PMP® is a registered certification mark of the Project Management Institute.

many of the world's largest corporations in such diverse industries as telecommunications, oil exploration and refining, financial services, and computer manufacturing.

ESI provides a variety of project management consulting services ranging from individual and organizational assessments, to methodology development, to hands-on coaching and mentoring.

Call 1-703-558-3020 for a catalog or visit our Web site at http://www.esi-intl.com.

Acknowledgments

I have always been fascinated with language. Perhaps this is so because of my legendary inability to learn any "foreign" language, although many people have tried to teach me. Nevertheless, I am to be envied, because I have a group of friends, colleagues, and professional acquaintances whose interest completely aligns with mine when it comes to the "language" of project management. Although not a "foreign" language per se, it does require study and experience in the field to comprehend the scope of the discipline. Accordingly, these friends and colleagues deserve special recognition for their valuable contribution in preparing this publication. It has been my pleasure and privilege to have worked side-by-side with each of them.

First, I must recognize my friend and colleague **Ginger Levin**, who continually amazes me with her insight and knowledge of the business and her never-ending creativity. She undertook the Herculean task of wading through hundreds of terms to ferret out those that were relevant for our first draft. Additionally, as a project management consultant and trainer for more than 22 years, she compiled glossaries from her own materials that she graciously shared for this work. Without Ginger's involvement, this publication would not have achieved the rich variety of terms it contains.

I would like to thank the **Technical Advisory Board,** a group of experienced practitioners whose depth of experience rivals that of any assemblage of professionals in the field. These individuals have managed projects of all types and complexities and have participated with ESI in project management consulting and training on six continents. Their studious review of and commentary on the terms included here ensure that we have not created a publication for its own sake, but for the explicit use of practitioners in the field.

Creating a glossary is harder than it looks. Describing the meaning of terms for an international audience requires the involvement of only the most experienced editor—one with a keen eye and deep appreciation for clear and precise exposition. **Dixie Richards**, senior editor, has collaborated with me now on several specialty publications that have enriched the literature in the field. Dixie not only has the substantive technical skills required to produce such publications, she brings to the task remarkable management skills in actually getting a book printed. I also appreciate the work of **Trinh Le**, whose document design skills were instrumental in updating and reformatting this second edition.

Finally, a special note of appreciation and thanks to the Project Management Institute for having laid the groundwork for this effort by identifying early on many of the terms they permitted us to incorporate in this glossary. Certainly, such inclusion enhances the value of this publication, which underscores PMI®'s overarching objective of advancing the art and science of project management worldwide.

Technical Advisory Board

Introduction

Whether you're looking for definitions of terms, phrases, or acronyms, you'll find them all arranged alphabetically in this handy tool. Each entry is succinctly defined and cross referenced, providing important insight into some aspect of project management.

Four types of references assist you in using the glossary to its fullest extent:

See references following acronyms direct you to the complete spelling and definition of the entry. You can find the definition of scores of acronyms, such as ACWP (actual cost of work performed) and PDCA (plan-do-check-act cycle).

See references following terms or phrases direct you to the more widely used terms or phrases and their full definitions. For example, if you look up responsibility matrix, you will be directed to responsibility assignment matrix for the full definition.

See also references following terms or phrases direct you to other entries that provide additional or comparative information. For example, when you look up the word acceptance, you'll find that it is one way of dealing with the consequences of a risk. But you'll also find a reference to the other two ways of dealing with the consequences of a risk: avoidance and mitigation. That means if you remember just one of the ways to deal with risk, the glossary will lead you to the others!

And finally, the *Also called* references following entries denote terms that are often used interchangeably, such as analogous estimating and top-down estimating.

For those of you studying for the PMP® certification exam, you will find the glossary an excellent study aid.

A

AACE
See American Association of Cost Engineers.

Abba chart
Graph (named for Wayne Abba) that is composed of four different indicators showing trends in historic and projected efficiency to date.

ABC
See activity-based costing.

ABM
See activity-based management.

acceptable quality level (AQL)
Maximum number of nonconforming items that can be included in an acceptable lot, usually expressed as a percentage. *See also* lot.

acceptance
Risk response strategy that prepares for and deals with the consequences of a risk, either actively (for example, by developing a contingency plan to execute if the risk event occurs) or passively (for example, by accepting a lower profit if some activities run over budget). *See also* avoidance *and* mitigation.

acceptance criteria
Requirements that a project or system must demonstrably meet before customers accept delivery.

acceptance review
Process by which a buyer or end-user determines that the item, product, or service presented for acceptance complies with its specification.

acceptance sampling

Statistical procedure used in quality control that involves testing a batch of products to determine whether the proportion of units having a particular attribute exceeds a given percentage. Sampling involves three determinations: batch size, sample size, and the maximum number of defects that will be allowed before rejecting the entire batch.

acceptance test procedure

Step-by-step set of instructions for the preparation and operation of the acceptance test, and the evaluation of the acceptance test results.

acceptance testing

Applying performance and capability measurements to project deliverables to ensure that they meet specifications and requirements and satisfy the customer.

accountability

(1) Total responsibility of an individual for the satisfactory completion of a specific assignment.
(2) State of assuming liability for something of value either through a contract or because of one's position of responsibility.

accountability matrix

See responsibility assignment matrix.

accounting period

Set period of time, usually one month, in which project costs and revenues are posted for information and analysis.

accounts payable

List of debts owed based on the purchase of services, inventory, supplies, and so on.

accounts receivable

List of monies due on current accounts based on the sale of products or services.

accreditation

Formal recognition granted by a regulatory board to an organization identifying it as being qualified to perform ISO 9000 quality system assessments of other organizations.

acid test

Most rigorous and severe form of testing for reliability, maintainability, and other criteria. Term is derived from the fact that gold resists acids that corrode other metals; the "acid test" was used to identify metals purporting to be gold.

acquisition

Obtaining supplies or services by and for the use of an organization through a purchase or lease, regardless of whether the supplies or services are already in existence or must be created, developed, demonstrated, or evaluated.

acquisition control

System for acquiring project equipment, material, and services in a uniform and orderly fashion and for managing that acquisition process.

acquisition methods

Ways in which goods or services are acquired from contractors, such as by sealed bid, competitive negotiation, and sole- or single-source award.

acquisition plan

Document that addresses all technical, business, management, and other significant considerations that will control an acquisition.

acquisition process

Process of acquiring goods or services for new or existing work.

action plan

Detailed document describing those project tasks that need to be done, when, and by whom.

active listening
Paying close attention to what is said, asking the other party to describe carefully and clearly what is meant, and requesting that ideas be repeated to clarify any ambiguity or uncertainty.

activity
Element of work that is required by the project, uses resources, and takes time to complete. Activities have expected durations, costs, and resource requirements and may be subdivided into tasks. *See also* task.

activity definition
Identification of specific activities that must be performed to produce the project deliverables. *Also called* activity description.

activity description
See activity definition.

activity duration
Best estimate of the time (hours, days, weeks, months, or, sometimes, years) needed to accomplish the work involved in an activity, considering the nature of the work and resources required for it.

activity duration estimating
Estimating the number of work periods needed to complete individual activities.

activity list
Enumeration of all the activities to be performed on the project. Organized as an extension to the WBS to ensure that all activities that are part of the project scope (and only those activities) are listed. Includes descriptions of each activity to ensure that project team members understand all the work that must be accomplished.

activity sequencing
Identifying and documenting activity dependencies.

activity-based costing (ABC)

Methodology that assigns costs to products or services based on the resources they consume. It assigns functional costs, direct and indirect, to the activities of an organization and then traces those activities to the product or service that caused the activities to be performed. ABC shows how effectively resources are being used and how all relevant activities contribute to the cost of a product or service. Such information may be key to making decisions about whether to restructure or privatize an activity.

activity-based management (ABM)

Approach to management that uses detailed economic analyses of important business activities to improve strategic and operational decisions. Attempts to increase the accuracy of cost information by more precisely allocating overhead and other indirect costs to products, projects, or customer segments. To successfully implement ABM, overhead and other indirect costs must be tracked by activity, which can then be traced to products, projects, or customers.

activity-on-arc

See precedence diagramming method.

activity-on-arrow (AOA)

See arrow diagramming method.

activity-on-node (AON)

See precedence diagramming method.

actual cost

(1) Amount a buyer pays to a seller for a product or service. It may be, but does not have to be, the same as market, insurable, or retail value.
(2) Cost a seller actually incurs to produce a product or provide a service, as distinguished from forecast final cost.

actual cost of work performed (ACWP)

Total costs (direct and indirect) incurred in accomplishing work during a given time period. *See also* earned value.

actual damages

Losses directly related to a breach or tortuous act that can readily be proven to have been sustained and for which the injured party should be compensated.

actual finish date

Point in time when work ended on an activity. In some cases, the activity may be considered "finished" when work is "substantially complete."

actual incurred rates

Rates that reflect actual expenditures as they have been recorded in the organization's accounting system.

actual start date

Point in time when work started on an activity.

ACV

See at-completion variance.

ACWP

See actual cost of work performed.

ADM

See arrow diagramming method.

administrative closure

Activities associated with generating, gathering, and disseminating information to formalize acceptance of the product or service of the project by the sponsor, client, or customer for a specific project phase or at project completion.

administrative expense

Expense that cannot be easily identified with a specific function or project but contributes in some way to the project or general business operations.

advance payment

Advance of money made by the buyer to the contractor before, in anticipation of, and applicable to performance under a contract.

affiliates
Associated business organizations or individuals if, directly or indirectly, (1) either one controls or can control the other or (2) a third party controls or can control both.

agreement
Mutual assent between two or more competent parties and usually reduced to writing in a contract.

allocable cost
Cost assignable or chargeable to one or more cost objectives as defined or agreed upon by the contractual parties.

allocated baseline
Baseline in which each function and subfunction of the product is allocated a set of performance and design requirements. These requirements are stated in sufficient detail for allocation to hardware, software, procedural data, facilities, and personnel.

allowable cost
Cost that can be recovered for the performance of a contract.

alternatives
Different means available to attain objectives.

alternatives analysis
Process of breaking down a complex situation to generate different solutions and approaches and evaluate the impact of trade-offs to attain objectives.

alternatives identification
Technique used to generate different approaches to completing the project.

ambiguity
Contract language that can be understood to have more than one reasonable meaning.

ambiguous jurisdictions

Potentially confusing situation in which two or more parties hold related responsibility for project work and their work boundaries and role definitions are unclear.

amendment

(1) Written, agreed upon, change to a legal document, usually a contract.

(2) Alteration to a solicitation.

American Association of Cost Engineers (AACE)

Professional organization that advances the science and art of cost engineering.

American National Standards Institute (ANSI)

Voluntary organization that helps set standards and also represents the United States in the International Standards Organization (ISO).

amortization

Accounting procedure that incrementally accounts for the cost or revenue value of a limited-life or intangible asset through periodic adjustments to income.

amount at stake

Extent of positive or adverse consequences that could occur to the project if a specific risk, or series of risks, occurs. The potential value (positive or negative) associated with a risk. *See also* project risk.

analogous estimating

Using the actual duration or cost of a previous, similar activity as the basis for estimating the duration or cost of a present or future activity; a form of expert judgment. *Also called* top-down estimating.

analysis

(1) Study and examination of something complex by separating it into more simple components. Typically, includes discovering the parts of the thing being studied, how they fit together, and why they are arranged in a particular way.

(2) Study of variances for cause, impact, corrective action, and results.

analytic approach
Process of breaking problems into their constituent parts to understand them better and, thereby, solve the problem.

annual basis
Statistical technique in which financial numbers for a period of less than 12 months are adjusted to an annual figure.

annual percentage rate
Cost of credit that consumers will pay over a 12-month period, expressed as a simple annual percentage.

annual receipts
Annual average gross revenue of an organization.

annual report
Formal financial statement containing a descriptive narrative of business operations for the year just ended. Issued by corporations for its shareholders, employees, and other interested parties.

ANSI
See American National Standards Institute.

anticipatory breach
Breaking a contract before the actual time of required performance wherein one party informs the other of its intentions not to fulfill its obligations.

AOA
See activity-on-arrow.

AON
See activity-on-node.

apparent low bidder

Prospective contractor who has submitted the lowest compliant bid for all or part of a project as described in a set of bid or tender documents.

application

(1) Act of putting to use new techniques or applying existing techniques to a project.

(2) Software program that carries out a task, or sequence of tasks, (for example, a database manager, spreadsheet, graphics program, or word processor).

application area

Category of projects with common elements not present in all projects; usually defined in terms of either the product of the project (that is, by similar technologies or industry sectors) or the type of customer (for example, internal versus external or government versus commercial).

application prototyping

Developing requirements dynamically rather than specifying all requirements at the outset of the project. Allows the customer to play an active role in defining the requirements as the project is being executed. *See also* rapid prototyping.

applied direct cost

Amount of money that is incurred during a given time period and is associated with the consumption of labor, material, and other direct resources, regardless of the date of commitment or date of payment.

applied rates

Rates used by internal management for budgeting and reporting for the current accounting period. Applied rates do not have to match the negotiated bidding rates; a conservative project manager or organization often sets them slightly above the bidding rates.

apportioned cost account

Cost account with a direct performance relationship to some other discrete activity, called the reference base. For example, assembly inspection normally has a direct relationship to assembly hours such that for every 200 hours of assembly, 25 hours of assembly inspection are required.

apportioned effort

Effort related to some other discrete or measurable effort, usually as a constant percent of the other effort but by itself not measurable as a work package, such as quality assurance or quality control.

approach

Overall method by which project objectives will be realized, including methodologies, life cycles, responsibilities, and other associated strategies, tactics, practices, and procedures.

approved bidders list

List of contractors that have been prequalified for the purpose of submitting competitive bids or tenders.

approved change

Change to the project scope, schedule, or budget that has been approved by higher authority.

AQL

See acceptable quality level.

arbitration

Formal system to deal with grievances and administer corrective justice as part of collective bargaining agreements. May be binding or nonbinding.

arbitrator

Impartial person who resolves a dispute or disagreement between two or more parties. In "binding" arbitration, the parties must accept the decision of the arbitrator.

arc

Line connecting two nodes.

arrow

In ADM, graphic presentation of an activity. The tail of the arrow represents the start of the activity; the head of the arrow represents the finish. Unless a time scale is used, the length of the arrow stem has no relation to the duration of the activity.

arrow diagramming method (ADM)

Network diagramming technique in which activities are represented by arrows. The tail of the arrow represents the start of the activity; the head of the arrow represents the finish of the activity. The length of the arrow does not represent the expected duration of the activity. Activities are connected at points called nodes (usually drawn as circles) to illustrate the sequence in which the activities are expected to be performed. *Also called* activity-on-arrow.

as-built schedule

Final project schedule showing actual start, duration, and finish dates. *Also called* as-performed schedule.

as-of date

See data date.

as-performed schedule

See as-built schedule.

asset

Amount recorded on a contractor's balance sheet representing the value of property owned by or debts owed to the contractor. May be cash, near-cash (accounts receivable, temporary investments, notes receivable), or nonmonetary property.

assignment of contract

Transfer of the rights and obligations under a contract to another party.

assumption

Factor that is considered to be true, real, or certain and is often used as a basis for decision making.

at-completion variance (ACV)
Difference between the budget at completion (BAC) and the estimate at completion (EAC).

attribute
Characteristic or property that is appraised in terms of whether it does or does not exist (for example, heads or tails on a coin) with respect to a given requirement.

attribute sampling
Statistical technique used to determine the quality, and therefore acceptance, of an item by inspecting samples of the larger population. An attribute may be a qualitative or quantitative characteristic of an item that is either met or not met according to the specifications.

audit
(1) Formal examination of a project's accounts or financial situation.
(2) Methodical examination of the project, either in whole or in part, usually conducted according to a pre-established schedule, to assess overall progress performance.

audit trail
Record of documentation describing actions taken, decisions made, and funds expended and earned on a project. Used to reconstruct the project after the fact for lessons learned and other purposes.

auditability
Capability of a project or portion of a project to undergo formal investigation of records relating to financial status or progress performance.

auditor
Person who conducts an audit.

Australian quality award
Award honoring the quality practices of Australian organizations. Based on a model certified by the Australian Quality Council, an organization recognized by the Australian

government as the preeminent authority on quality management. Seven categories of criteria are used by the council to determine the award winners: leadership; strategy, policy, and planning; information and analysis; people; customer focus; quality of process, product, and service; and organizational performance.

authoritarian management style

Management approach in which the project manager tells team members what is expected of them, provides specific guidance on what should be done, makes his or her role within the team understood, schedules work, and directs team members to follow standard rules and regulations.

authority

(1) Power or influence, either granted to or developed by individuals, that leads to others doing what those individuals direct.

(2) Formal conferment of such influence through an instrument such as a project charter.

authorize

Give final approval; a person who can authorize something is vested with authority to give final endorsement, which requires no further approval.

authorized unpriced work

Customer-authorized additions or deletions to the project scope (as described in the statement of work) that are being worked on by the project team prior to their being negotiated.

authorized work

Effort that has been approved by higher authority and may or may not be expressed in specific terms.

autocratic management style

Management approach in which the project manager makes all the decisions and exercises tight control over the project team. This style is usually characterized by communication from the project manager downward to the team and not vice versa.

average-sample-size curve
Plotted curve showing the average sample size that can be expected to occur under various sampling plans for a given quality process. *See also* sample size.

avoidance
Risk response strategy that eliminates the threat of a specific risk event, usually by eliminating its potential cause. The project management team can never eliminate all risk, but certain risk events often can be eliminated. *See also* acceptance *and* mitigation.

award
Notification by an organization that it will contract with another party. Usually is made by acceptance of an offer or tender that has been made by a contractor or seller.

award fee
Payment that the contractor receives above the base fee in a cost-plus-award fee (CPAF) contract. Total amount of fee available to be awarded is set forth in the original contract and should be an amount that is sufficient to provide motivation for excellence in such areas as quality, timeliness, technical ingenuity, and cost-effective management.

B

BAC
See budget at completion.

backcharge
Cost of corrective action taken by the buyer that is chargeable to the contractor under the terms of the contract.

backward pass
Calculation of late finish and late start dates for uncompleted portions of all network activities. Determined by working backward through the network logic from the project's end date. *See also* network analysis *and* forward pass.

BAFO
See best and final offer.

balance sheet
Financial statement that sets forth an organization's assets, liabilities, and net worth.

balanced matrix
Form of project organization in which the project manager's authority over project resources is roughly equal to that of the organization's functional managers.

balanced scorecard
Approach used to measure business performance. Developed by Robert Kaplan and David Norton, it includes not only financial performance but other elements such as customer value, internal business process, innovation, and employee performance. It is implemented by translating the organization's vision and strategy statements into a comprehensive and quantifiable set of objectives and performance measures, by obtaining organization-wide acceptance of the measures, by creating appropriate reward systems, and by collecting and analyzing performance results as they relate to the measures.

bar chart
See Gantt chart.

base fee
Fixed dollar amount established at the beginning of a cost-plus-award fee contract as the minimum amount of profit the contractor will receive, regardless of performance quality.

base pay rate
Amount of money paid to an employee on an hourly basis for regular or overtime work.

baseline
(1) Original plan (for a project, work package, or activity), plus or minus any approved changes. May be used with a modifier

(for example, cost baseline, schedule baseline, performance measurement baseline).
(2) Nominal plan to which deviations will be compared.

baseline finish date
Original planned finish date for a project, work package, or activity, plus or minus any approved changes.

baseline project plan
See project plan.

baseline start date
Original planned start date for a project, work package, or activity, plus or minus any approved changes.

batch
See lot.

BCR
See benefit-cost ratio.

BCWP
See budgeted cost of work performed.

BCWS
See budgeted cost of work scheduled.

benchmark
(1) Measured point of reference used to make comparisons.
(2) Test or tests conducted on computer hardware, software, or telecommunications equipment to determine that the configuration performs according to vendor-published performance specifications and satisfies certain functional requirements that are unable to be measured in terms of performance or design criteria.

benchmarking
(1) Comparing project practices to those of similar projects to provide a standard by which to measure performance.

(2) Conducting a test or tests on computer hardware, software, or telecommunications equipment to determine whether it meets certain requirements.

benefit

Gain to be accrued from the successful completion of a project. Benefits are compared to costs to ensure the selection of the most advantageous project or the most effective approach to complete a project.

benefit measurement methods

Comparative approaches, scoring models, benefit contributions, or economic models used for evaluating the positive aspects of projects.

benefit-cost analysis

Process of estimating tangible and intangible costs (outlays) and benefits (returns) of various project alternatives and using financial measures, such as return on investment or payback period, to evaluate the relative desirability of the alternatives.

benefit-cost ratio (BCR)

Financial measurement method used in project selection, it is one tool that is often used in a benefit-cost analysis. Requires that benefits, as well as costs, be quantified. Calculated by using the following formula: B/C. A BCR greater than one indicates that the value of the project's benefits are greater than its costs. For example, if we estimate benefits of $4 and costs of $2 (4/2), we will calculate a BCR of 2, or 2:1 indicating $2 of benefit for each dollar of cost. BCR does not provide profitability information, nor does it indicate magnitude of cost or benefit.

best and final offer (BAFO)

(1) Final offer by a contractor to perform the work after incorporating negotiated and agreed-upon changes in the bid or tender documents and any other changes to the prospective contractor's cost or technical proposal.

(2) Offer or tender submitted in a competitive negotiated procurement after written or oral discussions have been conducted.

best efforts
Contractual obligation to attempt to meet a goal, which requires contractors to use their best efforts to perform the work within the estimated contract cost and schedule.

beta test
Test of a product in its intended environment with the results used for their intended application.

biased sample
Sample that is neither truly representative nor random as a result of poor sampling procedures.

bid
(1) Offer to perform the work described in a set of bid or tender documents at a specified cost.
(2) Procurement or tender document generally used when the source selection decision will be determined based primarily on price. *See also* proposal *and* quotation.

bid bond
A legal instrument, obtained by the seller, and required by the buyer, that ensures the work will be performed even if the seller cannot complete the work. The company from whom the bid is obtained is legally liable for the performance of the contract and is called the guarantor.

bid cost considerations
Consideration of the contractor's approach, reasonableness of cost, cost realism, forecast of economic factors affecting cost, and cost risks used in the cost proposal.

bid guarantee
Form of security to ensure that the prospective contractor (1) will not withdraw a bid within the period specified for acceptance and (2) will execute a written contract and furnish

required bonds, including any necessary coinsurance or reinsurance agreements, during the time specified in the bid.

bid list
List of contractors invited to submit bids for goods or services as specified.

bid opening
Public opening of bids submitted in a sealed bid procurement.

bid protest
Process by which an unsuccessful contractor may seek a remedy for possibly unjust contract awards.

bid response
Communication, positive or negative, from prospective contractors in response to the invitation to bid.

bid sample
Sample to be furnished by a contractor to show the characteristics of its product offered in a bid.

bid/no bid
Decision point for management to either approve or disapprove the preparation of a proposal in response to a request for proposal, tender, invitation to bid, request for quotation, or any other vehicle by which a buyer solicits responses from a prospective seller.

bidder
One who submits a bid.

bidders conference
Meeting with prospective contractors prior to preparation of bids and proposals. Ensures that all prospective contractors have a clear and common understanding of the procurement or tender. *Also called* contractors conference, vendors conference, *or* prebid conference.

bidders list

List of suppliers judged capable by the buyer's organization from which bids, proposals, or quotations may be solicited. The list is developed and maintained by the buyer's organization. Verification of the suppliers' capability typically involves review of financial status and past performance, as well as on-site review of facilities and personnel.

bidding time

(1) Time allowed prospective contractors to prepare and submit their bids.
(2) Time between issuing the solicitation and opening the bids.

bilateral contract

Contract in which parties exchange promises to perform reciprocal obligations in the future. Contrasted with unilateral contracts, in which one party makes a promise in exchange for the performance of another party.

bill of lading

Document used to show receipt of goods for shipment issued by an organization in the business of transporting or forwarding goods (including airbills).

Bill of Materials (BOM)

(1) Set of physical elements required to build a project.
(2) Hierarchical view of the physical assemblies, subassemblies, and components needed to fabricate a manufacturing product.
(3) Descriptive and quantitative list of materials, supplies, parts, and components required to produce a designated complete end item of material, assembly, or subassembly.

bill of quantities

Project costing calculation completed before using a WBS and based on a per-component or per-project cost. Used widely in the construction industry.

binding arbitration

Arbitration in which parties are legally bound to the decision of the arbitrator. *See also* arbitration.

blue-ribbon committee

Group of experts who rigorously examine evidence, documents, and testimony to certify that a high-risk project has been properly planned, that risks have been quantified or otherwise adequately addressed, and that the probability of success is sufficient for the project to be funded or launched.

body language

Nonverbal communication, often unintended, from one party to another. Consists of facial expressions, physical stance and gestures, and any other physical expression that either complements or contradicts the spoken word. Body language often helps parties to a discussion better understand the real meaning of the spoken word.

boilerplate

Standard and essential contract terminology and clauses that are not subject to frequent change. Use of the term can be dangerous because it may lull contract parties into thinking they need not read the clauses, assuming no changes from previous contracts, or assuming the data are not significant.

BOM

See Bill of Materials.

bond

Written instrument executed by an offeror or contractor (the principal) and a second party (the surety or sureties) to ensure fulfillment of the principal's obligations to a third party identified in the bond. Reimbursement of any loss sustained by the obligee if the principal's obligations are not met is ensured to the extent stipulated in the bond.

bonus

Extra compensation paid to an employee or contractor, usually for superior performance.

bottleneck

Process constraint that determines the capacity or capability of a system and restricts the rate, volume, or flow of a process.

bottom-up budget

See bottom-up estimating.

bottom-up estimating

Cost or budget estimate derived by first estimating the cost of the project's elemental tasks at the lower levels of the WBS and then aggregating those estimates at successively higher levels of the WBS. The project manager typically includes indirect costs, general and administrative expenses, profit, and any reserves when calculating the total project cost estimate. *See also* definitive estimate.

brainstorming

Problem-solving technique that can be used for planning purposes, risk identification, improvement efforts, and other project-related endeavors. Participants are invited to share their ideas in a group setting, where no disapproving verbal or nonverbal behaviors are permitted. The technique is designed to generate a large number of ideas by helping people to think creatively and allowing them to participate fully, without feeling inhibited or criticized by others.

breach

Failure to perform a contractual obligation. *See also* material breach.

breach of contract

(1) Failure, without legal excuse, to perform any promise that forms any part of a contract. Applies to both express promises in a contract and implied promises that are inherent in the transaction.
(2) Unequivocal, distinct, and absolute refusal to perform under the contract.

breakdown

Identification of the smallest activities or tasks in a project for estimating, monitoring, and controlling purposes.

break-even chart

Graphic representation of the relationship between total value earned and total costs for various levels of production, plotted on a time or volume scale.

break-even point

Point in time during project or production performance at which value earned equals total cost.

budget

Quantitative expression of management's plans to perform specified work. Used to present management's intentions and objectives to all levels of the organization, monitor implementation of the plans, and provide a quantitative basis for measuring and rewarding individual and unit performance.

budget at completion (BAC)

Sum of approved cost estimates (including any overhead allocation) for all activities in a project. *See also* earned value.

budget costs

(1) Translation of the work estimate into hourly rates, quantity units of production, and the like. Used for comparison to actual costs to determine variances, evaluate performance, and alert those responsible to implement corrective action as needed.
(2) Assigned expenditure plan for specified cost elements.

budget decrement

Amount of a reduction in available funds for an activity.

budget estimate

Estimate of the funds needed to obtain project approval, which includes a combination of fixed and unit prices for labor, material, equipment, and other direct and indirect costs.

budget update

Change to an approved cost baseline, generally revised only in response to scope changes.

budgeted cost of work performed (BCWP)
Sum of approved cost estimates (including any overhead allocation) for activities (or portions of activities) completed during a given period. *See also* earned value.

budgeted cost of work scheduled (BCWS)
Sum of approved cost estimates (including any overhead allocation) for activities (or portions of activities) scheduled to be performed during a given period. *See also* earned value.

bulk material
(1) Material bought in lots; generally, no specific item is distinguishable from any other in the lot.
(2) Items that may be purchased from a standard catalog description and are bought in quantity to be distributed as needed.

burden
See indirect cost.

bureaucratic authority
Influence derived from an individual's knowing the organization's rules, regulations, and procedures and the ways to use them to obtain desired results in an expedient and expeditious manner.

burn rate
Rate at which funds are expended on a project (for example, total dollars per day or total dollars per week). Usually quoted based on labor hours only, but may include materials as well.

business agreement
Commitment to perform a task or series of tasks to accomplish objectives leading to a deliverable or completion of a project.

business case
See project business case.

business process model
Decomposition and graphical depiction of a specific business process or functional area within an organization. The model

shows how each functional area breaks down into processes; each process breaks down into subprocesses; and each subprocess breaks down into activities.

business process reengineering
Method to improve organizational performance by evaluating and redesigning business processes.

business risk
Risk—with its inherent potential for either profit or loss—that is associated with any particular endeavor.

buying in
Submitting or tendering an offer below anticipated costs with the expectation of increasing the contract amount after award, for example, through unnecessary or excessively priced contract modifications.

C

C/SCS
See cost/schedule control system.

C/SCSC
See cost/schedule control system criteria.

C/SSR
See cost/schedule status report.

CAD
See computer-aided design.

calendar
Tool used to identify project workdays in developing a project plan. Can be altered so that weekends, holidays, weather days, religious festivals, and so on are not included as project workdays.

calendar range

Span of the calendar from the calendar start date, or unit number one, through the last calendar unit to be performed.

calendar start date

First calendar unit of the working calendar.

calendar unit

Smallest unit of time used in scheduling the project, generally expressed as hours, days, or weeks, but also can be in shifts or even minutes. Used primarily in specific project management software packages.

Canadian quality award

Originally introduced in 1984 as the Canada Awards for Business Excellence, the award was revised to reflect the conceptual structure of the U.S. government's Malcolm Baldrige National Quality Award and released in 1989. The National Quality Institute of Canada, which administers the award, uses it to recognize Canadian organizations that successfully practice continuous quality improvement. The award relies on the The Roadmap to Excellence guide, which identifies the following 10 steps to continuous improvement: support the quality principles; reward the quality criteria; take quality tests; develop an improvement plan; spread the quality message; enact the improvement program; monitor the improvement plan; retest for quality; maintain gains; and continuous improvement.

capability maturity model

Model used to describe the relative maturity of an organization, or subset of an organization, with respect to processes such as software engineering, product development, people development, systems integration, or project management, among others. Usually consists of five maturity levels that have been described as end-state conditions. The current practice of an organization is compared to the model from which a determination is made as to which of the five levels the organization's practices represent. This information is then used to guide the organization into establishing action plans to advance to the next level. The first and perhaps best known capability maturity model was developed by the Software Engineering Institute for software engineering processes. It remains, to this day, the "gold standard" of maturity models. In project management, ESI has developed ProjectFramework, a maturity model for project management processes.

capability validation

Technical verification of the ability of a proposed automated data processing system configuration, replacement component, or software to satisfy functional requirements.

capital

In finance, money and any other property of an organization used in transacting its business.

capital assets

Physical property of an organization that generally has long, useful life such as equipment, vehicles, or buildings.

capital expenditure

Money paid for improvements that will have a life of more than 1 year.

capitalization

Treatment of expenditures as assets rather than current expenses. Under general accounting practices in certain countries, contractors are required to capitalize costs of tangible assets when they exceed predetermined amounts.

career path planning

Process of integrating an individual's career planning and development into the organization's personnel plans, with the objective of satisfying the organization's requirements and the individual's career goals.

CASE tools

See computer-aided software engineering tools.

cash flow
The amounts, sources, and uses of cash in an organization.

cash-flow analysis
Establishment of the source and application of funds by time period and the accumulated total cash flow for the project to measure actual versus budget costs. Needed for determining the project's funding requirements at the lowest carrying charges and used to measure progress of the project.

category of material
Particular type of goods, acquired or produced by a contractor, that consists of identical or interchangeable units and is intended to be sold, consumed, or used during project performance.

cause-and-effect diagram
See Ishikawa diagram.

CCB
See change control board.

cellular processing
Technique used to design, group, and manage production operations as self-contained flexible cells capable of start-to-finish in processing a group of items.

center of excellence
See project office (1).

center of expertise
See project office (1).

centralized contracting
Single function responsible for the entire contracting process. Person in charge of this function is accountable to management for the proper performance of contracting activities.

CER
See cost estimating relationship.

certification

(1) Assessment by an independent, accredited third party to confirm a quality system's conformance to the ISO 9000 or other series of standards.

(2) Signed representation that certain facts are accurate.

champion

(1) Person who spearheads an idea or action and promotes it throughout the organization.

(2) Person with significant influence who takes personal responsibility (although usually not for day-to-day management) for the successful completion of a project for the organization.

chance

Possibility of an indicated outcome in an uncertain situation. *See also* probability.

change

(1) Increase or decrease in any project characteristics—time, cost, or technical requirements.

(2) Deviation from agreed-upon specifications, definition, functionality, or plans; alternate approach to project work accomplishments.

(3) Alteration in a contract as permitted by a contract clause.

change control

(1) Process of monitoring and dealing with changes to the schedule, cost, or scope of a project, or its overall objectives. May be considered a subset of configuration management.

(2) Defined process and procedure for change management during the project life cycle.

change control board (CCB)

Formally constituted group of stakeholders responsible for approving or rejecting changes to the project baselines. *Also called* configuration control board.

change control procedure
Process for initiating changes to the project baseline configuration; analyzing the impact of changes to project cost, schedule, and scope; approving or disapproving changes; and updating project or product specifications and baselines.

change control system
Collection of formal, documented procedures that defines the steps by which official project documents may be changed.

change management
(1) *See* configuration control.
(2) Process used to introduce, train, and implement a new system or set of procedures (the "change") in an organization so that the users or beneficiaries of the change assimilate it into their everyday work life. Change management is basically a process of acculturation.

change management plan
(1) Premeditated, documented approach to implementing configuration control.
(2) Approach used to assimilate a new system or set of procedures in an organization.

change order
Written directive issued by the buyer requiring the contractor to make changes according to the provisions of the contract document.

change request
(1) Request for modification to the terms of the contract or to the description of the product or service to be provided.
(2) Formal written statement asking to make a modification to a deliverable.

changed conditions
Change in the contract environment, physical or otherwise, from what was contemplated at the time of bid causing the seller to seek additional monies or time from the buyer to complete the contract requirement.

charismatic authority
Influence derived from an individual's personality. People do what is asked of them because they like the asker.

chart of accounts
Numbering system used to identify and monitor project costs by category (for example, labor, supplies, or materials). Usually, based on the corporate chart of accounts of the performing organization. *See also* code of accounts.

charter
See project charter.

checklist
Structured tool, usually industry or activity specific, used to direct that a set of required steps be performed.

claim
Written demand or assertion by one of the contracting parties seeking the payment of money, a change in interpretation of contract terms, or other relief arising under or relating to the contract.

clarification
Communication with a potential contractor on a competitively negotiated procurement for the purpose of eliminating minor irregularities, informalities, or apparent clerical mistakes in a proposal.

classification of risks
Process used to allocate responsibility for risks and identify causes and potential control mechanisms.

clearance number
Number of successively inspected units that must be found free of defects before a certain action to change the inspection procedure can be taken.

client
Customer, principal, owner, promoter, buyer, or end user of the product or service created by the project.

client quality services
Creation of a mutual feedback system between buyer and seller to define expectations, opportunities, and anticipated needs.

closeout phase
Fourth phase in the generic project life cycle where all outstanding contractual issues are completed and documented in preparation for turning over the product or service to the customer.

closing processes
Activities associated with formal acceptance of the phase or project and bringing it to an orderly end.

COCOMO
See constructive cost model.

code of accounts
Numbering system used to uniquely identify each element of the WBS. *See also* chart of accounts.

code of ethics
Written statement of principles addressing the behavior of the individuals employed in an organization.

coercive authority
Influence predicated on fear. People do what is asked of them because they fear the consequences if they do not.

collaboration software
Generic term used to describe any electronic and automated application that facilitates communication, trust, and teamwork among a group of people, usually a project team, who work on common tasks or objectives and who are not physically colocated. Examples include such common applications as e-mail and bulletin boards as well as more sophisticated examples such as electronic (that is, Web) conferences and meetings, Webcasts, electronic whiteboards, and instant messaging. Although many of these applications are Internet-based, they do not have to be to fit the definition.

collective bargaining agreement

Contractual agreement with unions or other employee groups.

colocation

Placement of project team members in the same physical location to enhance their ability to perform as a team.

combative management style

Management approach in which the project manager displays an eagerness to fight or be disagreeable over any given situation.

command failure

Failure of a system because of incorrect commands or signals from the operator or from other components.

commercial off the shelf (COTS)

Item, software application, or service available in the commercial market.

commissioning

(1) Process of substantiating the capability of the project to function as designed.
(2) Activity on a project that encompasses the on-site validation and refinement of the hardware deliverables.

commitment

(1) Agreement to consign or reserve the necessary resources to fulfill a requirement, until an expenditure occurs.
(2) State of being personally bound to something because of a delegation process or assignment and acceptance.
(3) Approved schedule or budget allowances where time, funding, and resources are formally allocated to an effort.

commodity

Tangible good or product.

common cause variation

Underlying reasons for the natural variation in a product or the delivery of a service resulting in minor deviations from the specifications or control limits. *See also* special cause variation.

communicating
Exchanging information.

communication
Effective transfer of information from one party to another; exchanging information between individuals through a common system of symbols, signs, or behavior. Communication comprises four elements: (1) communicator or sender of a message, (2) message, (3) medium of the message, and (4) receiver of the message.

communication barrier
Impediment to effective communication. Barriers may be physical, environmental, cultural, temporal, psychological, emotional, linguistical, or from any other source that diminishes the transmission and receipt of a message.

communication blocker
Negative reaction or response to a comment, suggestion, idea, or recommendation that has the effect of diminishing and impeding the communication exchange between the sender and recipient of a message. The sender typically holds the opinion that the recipient summarily dismissed the message content without giving it the level of consideration necessary.

communication channel
Means of communication used to transmit a message. Three communication channels exist in the project environment: (1) formal—communication within the organization's formal communication structure used to transmit policies, goals, and directives; (2) informal—communication outside the organization's formal communication structure; and (3) unofficial—interpersonal communication within the organization's social structure.

communication management plan
Document that describes the methods for gathering, distributing, and storing various types of information; provides a production schedule showing when each type of information will be produced; details methods for accessing information

between scheduled communications; and incorporates procedures for updating and refining the communication plan. Generally, a part of the overall project plan.

communication model

Communication process involving four parts: (1) communicator or sender—the originator of the message, (2) message—that which is to be conveyed (thoughts, feelings, or ideas), (3) medium—the vehicle or method used to convey the message, and (4) recipient—the person to whom the message is sent.

communication planning

Process used to identify the general or specific information needs of the project stakeholders, the frequency with which the information is presented to them, and the form the communication will take. Also includes general communication such as press releases, articles, and public presentations.

communication requirements

Total information needs of project stakeholders. Information necessary for determining project communication requirements includes (1) project organization and stakeholder responsibility relationships; (2) disciplines, departments, and specialties involved in the project; (3) number of individuals involved in the project and their locations; and (4) external information needs (such as communicating with the media).

communication skills

Methods, techniques, procedures, processes, and actions employed by the sender to ensure that the information transmitted is clear and complete and that it has been properly understood.

communication technology

Methods used to transfer information among project elements.

comparability

Condition that exists when an offered price can be compared with some other price for analysis. Exists when all price-related differences have been identified and accounted for so that the prices being compared are based on relatively equal assumptions.

compensable delay

Delay incurred by a contractor in contract performance for which the buyer must give compensation.

compensation and evaluation

Measurement of an individual's performance (evaluation) and the financial payment provided as a reward for that performance (compensation).

compensatory time

Time off granted to an employee at the discretion of the employer for overtime work or other noteworthy deed. *Also called* comp time.

competency

Critical skill, or in some cases personality characteristic, required of an individual to complete an activity or project, or otherwise required for a certain position. For example, the ability to think strategically is considered by some to be a critical competency for a person who will be the project manager of a large and complex project

competition

Effort of prospective suppliers of products or services to independently secure the business of the buyer by proposing the most attractive contract terms or by offering the highest quality service or product. Competition in relation to U.S. government activities is usually categorized in three ways: (1) public versus private, in which public-sector organizations compete with the private sector to conduct public-sector business; (2) public versus public, in which public-sector organizations compete among themselves to conduct public-sector business; and (3) private versus private, in which private-sector organizations compete among themselves to conduct public-sector business.

competitive advantage
Advantage of one competitor over another.

competitive benchmarking
Measuring products, services, and processes against those of other organizations engaged in the same business. *See also* benchmarking.

competitive negotiation
Method of acquisition that allows flexible procedures, permits bargaining, and provides an opportunity for prospective contractors to revise their offers before contract award.

competitive proposals
Procedure used by the U.S. federal government in negotiated procurement that (1) is initiated by an RFP, which sets out the requirements and the criteria to evaluate offers, (2) includes review of submitted proposals for conformance to requirements or specifications, price, and other factors, (3) usually provides for discussion or negotiation with those prospective contractors found to be within the competitive range, and (4) concludes with the award of a contract to the prospective contractor whose offer is most advantageous considering price and other factors included in the solicitation.

completed activity
Activity with an actual finish date and no remaining duration.

complexity estimate
Numerical prediction of the probable number of related factors that cause projects to be viewed as complex.

compliance
(1) Adhering to any standards, procedures, or processes established as necessary for operational effectiveness.
(2) Meeting all technical, contractual, and price/cost requirements of a request for proposal.

compound interest
Interest earned on principal plus interest earned in a preceding period.

compromising
See conflict resolution.

computer program
Series of instructions or statements, in a form acceptable to a computer, that are designed to cause the computer to execute an operation or operations.

computer software
Programs, procedures, rules, or routines specifically designed to make use of and extend the capabilities of computer equipment.

computer-aided design (CAD)
Computer system and related software with sophisticated graphics capability that are used to design machinery, buildings, local area networks, computer chips, and the like.

computer-aided software engineering (CASE) tools
Set of computer programs designed to improve and automate the software development process.

concept
Imaginative arrangement of a set of ideas.

concept phase
First of four sequential phases in the generic project life cycle where the idea or notion for a project is first articulated. *Also called* idea, economic analysis, feasibility, *or* prefeasibility phase.

conceptual development
Process of selecting and documenting the best approach for achieving project objectives.

conceptual estimate
See order-of-magnitude estimate.

conceptual solution

Initial technical approach developed to satisfy project requirements as they are known early in the project.

concern

(1) Problem, expressed because of lack of information about skills, resources, equipment, and facilities, that may turn into a risk if neglected. Often resolved as the infrastructure and facilities requirements are put in place.
(2) Business entity organized for profit.

conciliatory management style

Management approach in which the project manager is friendly and agreeable and attempts to unite all project parties involved to provide a compatible working team.

concurrent engineering

Approach to project staffing that calls for implementors to be involved in the design phase. Originally, use of a design team that included both design and manufacturing engineers, and later expanded to include staff from quality control, purchasing, and other relevant areas to accelerate project completion. Often confused with fast-tracking.

conditional diagramming method

Diagramming techniques, such as GERT or system dynamic models, that allow nonsequential activities such as loops or conditional branches.

configuration control

Process of maintaining the baseline identification and monitoring all changes to that baseline. Prevents unnecessary or marginal changes to the project scope while expediting the approval and implementation of changes that are considered needed or that offer significant project benefits.

configuration control board

See change control board.

configuration identification

Process of establishing and documenting an initial project baseline. Provides a systematic determination of all technical documentation needed to describe the functional and physical characteristics of items designated for configuration management to ensure that these documents are current, approved, and available for use at the needed time.

configuration item

Element of a configuration that is subject to configuration management.

configuration management

(1) Process used to apply technical and administrative direction to document the functional and physical characteristics of an item or system, control any changes to the characteristics, record and report the changes and their implementation status, and audit the item or system to verify conformance to requirements.

(2) Approach used to control changes to these characteristics and provide information on the status of engineering or contract change actions. Comprises three major areas of effort: configuration identification, configuration status accounting, and configuration control.

configuration status accounting

(1) Process of recording and documenting changes to an approved baseline to maintain a record of the status of the system components. Shows actions required and engineering changes completed.

(2) Identifies all configuration items of the initially approved configuration and then continually tracks authorized changes to the baseline.

conflict

Opposition resulting from incompatible expectations.

conflict management

Process by which an individual uses managerial techniques to deal with disagreements, both technical and personal in nature, that develop among the individuals working on the project.

conflict resolution

Process of seeking a solution to a problem. Generally, five methods are available: (1) problem solving or confrontation, where two parties work together toward a solution of the problem, (2) compromising, where both sides agree such that each wins or loses on certain significant issues, (3) forcing, where the project manager uses his or her power to direct the solution, resulting in a type of win-lose agreement where one side gets its way and the other does not, (4) smoothing, where the major points of agreement are given the most attention and differences between the two sides are not highlighted and are thus not resolved, and (5) withdrawing, where one or both sides withdraw from conflict.

confrontation

Also called problem solving. *See* conflict resolution.

consensual management style

Management approach in which the project manager presents problems to team members for discussion or input and encourages them to make decisions. This approach results in an increase in team member commitment to the group decision but also in the amount of time required to reach that decision.

consequential damages

Losses, injuries, or damages that do not flow directly and immediately from the act of a party but instead from some of the consequences or results of that party's act. Any such damages resulting from a seller's breach of contract, for example, including (1) any loss resulting from general or particular requirements and needs that the seller at the time of contracting had reason to know of and that could not reasonably be prevented and (2) any injury to people or property proximately resulting from any breach of warranty.

consideration

Inducement to a contract—the cause, motive, price, or impelling influence that leads a party to enter a contract. Generally requires two elements: (1) something must be given that the law regards as sufficient legal value for the purpose, either a benefit to the seller or a detriment to the buyer; and (2) the something (benefit or detriment of legal value) must be dealt with by the parties as the agreed-upon price or exchange for the promise.

constrained optimization methods

See project selection methods.

constraint

(1) Restriction that affects the scope of the project, usually with regard to availability, assignment, or use of project cost, schedule, or resources.

(2) Any factor that affects when or how an activity can be scheduled.

(3) Any factor that limits the project team's options and can lead to pressure and resulting frustrations among team members.

construction management

Process by which a potential owner of a capital facility engages a professional agent, called a construction manager, to coordinate, communicate, and direct the construction process in terms of scope, quality, time, and cost.

constructive cost model (COCOMO)

Software cost and schedule estimating model originally developed by Barry Boehm. Used for estimating the number of person months required to develop the most common type of software product and expressed as the number of thousands of delivered source instructions. Three levels of complexity: Basic, Intermediate, and Detailed. Principal difference among the three is the detail and quantity of information required to complete the estimate. Using the Detailed version, the estimator must consider, and assign a value to, the impact of fourteen specific cost drivers related to the software product to be developed. Model is derived from a study of 63 software projects and is nonproprietary.

consultant

Technical expert, subject matter expert, or solution specialist hired for a particular aspect of the project.

consultative-autocratic management style

Management approach in which extensive information input is solicited from team members, but the project manager makes all substantive decisions.

contingency

(1) Provision for any project risk elements within the project scope; particularly important when comparison of estimates and actual data suggests that certain risk events are likely to occur. If an allowance for escalation is included in the contingency, such should be a separate item, calculated to fit expected price level escalation conditions for the project.
(2) Possible future action that may stem from presently known causes, the cost outcome of which cannot be determined accurately. *See also* reserve *and* contingency plan.

contingency allowance

See contingency reserve.

contingency plan

Plan that identifies alternative strategies to be used if specified risk events occur. Examples include a contingency reserve in the budget, alternative schedule activity sequences, and emergency responses to reduce the impacts of risk events.

contingency planning

Process of producing a contingency plan. Occurs at the outset of the project and is a continuous process throughout the project life cycle.

contingency reserve

Quantity of money or time that is intended to reduce the impact of missed cost, schedule, or performance objectives, which can be only partly planned (sometimes called "known unknowns"), and that is normally included in the project's cost and schedule baseline.

continuous improvement process

(1) Process by which organizations continuously improve their processes and procedures to meet or exceed customer requirements.

(2) Means through which an organization creates and sustains a culture of continuous improvement.

contract

(1) Mutually binding agreement that obligates the seller to provide the specified product or service and obligates the buyer to pay for it.

(2) Legal relationship subject to remedy in a court. Generally, contracts fall into one of three broad categories: fixed-price or lump-sum; cost-reimbursement; and unit-price.

contract administration

Management of the relationship with the contractor from contract award to closeout, focused specifically on ensuring that the contractor delivers a product or service in conformance with the contract's requirements.

contract award

Acceptance of a final offer usually by issuing a purchase order or signing a legally binding contract formalizing the terms under which the goods or services are to be supplied.

contract budget base

Value of all negotiated contract costs, plus the estimated cost of authorized unpriced work.

contract change control system

Process by which the contract may be modified including the documentation, tracking systems, dispute resolution procedures, and approval levels necessary for authorizing change.

contract closeout

(1) Completion and settlement of the contract, including resolution of all outstanding items.

(2) Activities that ensure that the contractor has fulfilled all contractual obligations and has released all claims and liens in connection with the work performed.

contract dates

Times specified in the contract that define and impact the project schedule.

contract dispute

Disagreement between the contracting parties, which may occur during contract execution or at completion, may include misinterpretation of any technical requirements or terms and conditions, and may result from changes not anticipated at the time of contract award.

contract documents

Set of documents that forms the contract. Includes but is not limited to the contract itself, along with all supporting schedules; requested and approved contract changes; any contractor-developed technical documentation, contractor performance reports, and financial documents such as invoices and payment records; and the results of any contract-related inspections.

contract financial control

Control exercised over contract costs by the buyer or the contractor.

contract funds status report

In U.S. federal government procurement, document, normally prepared quarterly, that forecasts the funds required to complete the project, displaying them at the price level (cost + fee).

contract guarantee

Legally enforceable assurance of performance of a contract by a contractor.

contract modification
Written order authorizing the contractor to make changes according to the provisions of the contract documentation.

contract negotiations
Method of procurement in which a contract results from a bid that may be changed through bargaining. Involves clarification and mutual agreement on the structure and requirements of the contract prior to signing it.

contract pricing
Efforts involved in determining a specific pricing arrangement. Includes price analysis, cost analysis, and the use of accounting and technical evaluations and systems-analysis techniques to facilitate negotiation of realistic pricing arrangements.

contract quality requirements
Technical contract requirements concerning the quality of the product or service and contract clauses prescribing inspection and other quality controls incumbent on the contractor to ensure that the product or service conforms to the technical requirements.

contract risk
Risk, from either a buyer's or seller's perspective, that is related to a contract, including the level of risk borne by the buyer or seller as a result of the contract type.

contract risk analysis
Assessment of the probability that certain risk events will occur and of the consequences of such events on attaining the contract objectives.

contract target cost
Total anticipated value of all the negotiated costs in a contract, excluding fee and authorized unpriced work.

contract work breakdown structure (CWBS)
Tool used to describe the total product and work to be done to satisfy a specific contract. Normally prepared by a contractor to reflect the statement of work in a specific contract or request

for proposal. Used to define the level of reporting the
contractor will provide the buyer. *See also* work breakdown
structure.

contracting out

Term used in U.S. government contracting for the hiring of
private-sector firms or nonprofit organizations to provide
goods or services for the government. With this approach, the
government remains the financier, has management and policy
control over the type and quality of goods or services
provided, and can replace contractors that do not perform well.
See also outsourcing.

contractor

Person or organization undertaking responsibility for the
performance of a contract. *See also* supplier.

contractor performance evaluation

Comprehensive review of the contractor's technical
performance, cost performance, and work delivery schedule.

contractor qualification

Review of experience, past performance, capabilities,
resources, and current work loads of potential contractors.

contractor technical evaluation

Comprehensive review of the contractor's technical
competency, understanding of the technical requirements, and
capability to produce technically acceptable goods or services.

contractors conference

See bidders conference.

control

(1) Process of comparing actual performance with planned
performance, analyzing variances, evaluating alternatives, and
taking corrective action as needed.
(2) One of the key risk response strategies, calling for reduction
of the probability of a risk, reduction of the risk's impact, or
deflection of the risk to another party. *Also called* mitigation.

control chart

Graphic display of the results of a process over time and against established control limits. Used to determine whether the process is "in control" or "out of control," thereby requiring adjustment.

control gate

Specific point in time during the project life cycle (for example, beginning or end of a major phase, expenditure of a specific amount of money, specific results of a set of tests, and so on) at which key project stakeholders convene to assess performance to date, validate key project assumptions, analyze current and future market conditions, and discuss other factors to determine whether the project should—(1) be terminated, (2) proceed according to its original plan, or (3) proceed based on a revised plan. *Also called* phase exit, stage gate, kill point, or phase-end review.

control limits

Bounds beyond which unacceptable performance is indicated. Two control limits are used in statistical process control: upper control limit and lower control limit, and they are established as 3 standard deviations (SD) from the mean of the sample taken.

control system

See change control system.

controlling processes

Actions taken by the project team to ensure that project objectives are met, by monitoring and measuring progress and taking corrective action when needed.

controls

See project management controls.

conversion

Process of moving data, information, and programs from the current system to the new, or target, system. Conversion approaches include direct, parallel, phased, and pilot.

coordination
Orchestration of stakeholder actions and project events to achieve project objectives.

copyright
Protection granted to authors and artists prohibiting others from reproducing their works without their permission.

corporate culture
Organizational rules, rituals, procedures, ethics, values, mores, and general operating principles that all members of the group are expected to practice, if not endorse. All encompassing and generally differentiates one organization from another. Difficult to change and can be done only with great thought and tenacity on the part of management.

correction
Elimination of a defect.

corrective action
Changes made to bring expected future performance of the project in line with the project plan.

cost
(1) Cash value of project activity; value associated with materials and resources expended to accomplish project objectives.
(2) Sum or equivalent that is expended, paid, or charged for something.

cost account
(1) Defined work element or category for which actual costs can be accumulated and compared to BCWP.
(2) Cost category that represents the work assigned to one responsible organizational unit on a CWBS.

cost account matrix
Chart or conversion table that relates costs to the functional organizations and WBS elements.

cost accounting practice

Disclosed or established accounting method or technique used to measure cost; determine the amount of cost to be assigned to individual cost accounting periods; and allocate costs, directly and indirectly, to cost objectives.

cost analysis

Process used to develop or assess the reasonableness and validity of estimates and resource requirements by estimating the subelements of cost to produce an item or deliver a service. Includes a statement or report of the assessment and related conclusions.

cost baseline

Time-phased budget used to measure and monitor cost performance on the project. Developed by summing estimated costs by period and usually displayed in the form of an S-curve.

cost budgeting

Allocating cost estimates to individual project components.

cost center

Subdivision of an activity for which identification of costs is desired and through which costs can be controlled through one responsible manager.

cost change control system

Procedure by which the cost baseline may be changed, including documentation, tracking systems, and approval levels needed to authorize changes.

cost contract

Cost-reimbursement contract in which the contractor receives no fee or profit.

cost control

Oversight of changes to the project budget. Includes influencing the factors that cause changes to the cost baseline, determining that the cost baseline has changed, ensuring that the changes are beneficial, and managing actual changes when and as they occur.

cost controls
Processes and tools used to practice cost control, such as variance analysis, integrated cost and schedule reporting, progress analysis, and corrective action.

cost estimate
(1) Prediction of the expected monetary cost required to perform a task or acquire an item.
(2) Quantitative assessment of the likely costs of the resources required to complete project activities. May constitute a single value or a range of values and is based on understanding at a specific point in time.

cost estimating
Process of estimating the cost of the resources needed to complete project activities. Includes an economic evaluation, an assessment of project investment cost, and a forecast of future trends and costs.

cost estimating relationship (CER)
Mathematical relationship that defines cost as a function of one or more noncost parameters, such as performance, operating characteristics, or physical characteristics.

cost forecasting
Process of predicting future trends and costs throughout the project.

cost input
Cost, except for general and administrative expenses, that for contract costing purposes is allocable to the production of goods and services during a cost accounting period.

cost management
Function required to maintain effective financial control of the project by evaluating, estimating, budgeting, monitoring, analyzing, forecasting, and reporting cost information.

cost management plan
Document that describes how cost variances will be managed (for example, different responses for major and minor variances). May be part of the overall project plan.

cost objective
Function, organizational subdivision, contract, or other work unit for which cost data are desired and for which provision is made to accumulate and measure the cost of processes, products, jobs, capitalized projects, and the like.

cost of capital
Rate of return a corporation (or individual) could earn if it invested its capital in another investment, venture, or project with equivalent risk.

cost of quality
Costs incurred or expended to ensure quality, including those associated with the cost of conformance and nonconformance.

cost or pricing data
In U.S. federal government procurement, facts on the price of a contract (or the price of a contract modification), as of the date of agreement, that are expected to affect price negotiations significantly.

cost overrun
Amount by which actual project costs exceed estimated costs.

cost performance index (CPI)
Ratio of budgeted costs to actual costs (BCWP/ACWP). Often used to predict the amount of a possible cost overrun or underrun using the following formula: BAC ÷ CPI = EAC. *See also* earned value.

cost performance measurement baseline
Budget costs and measurable goals (particularly time and quantities) formulated for comparisons, analyses, and forecasts of future costs.

cost performance report (CPR)
Written account of cost and schedule progress and earned value, normally prepared monthly.

cost risk
(1) Risk associated with failing to complete tasks within the estimated budget allowances.
(2) Assessment of possible monetary loss or gain from the work to be done on a project.

cost underrun
Excess of a project's estimated costs over the actual cost for work that was within the project's scope.

cost variance (CV)
(1) Difference between the estimated and actual costs of an activity.
(2) In earned value, the numerical difference between BCWP and ACWP.

cost/schedule control system (C/SCS)
Management system requiring the contractor to establish a WBS for all the work to be performed on the contract and to record performance and costs for each element of that structure. Tracks the contractor's performance at a level of detail that will provide early information if the contractor is not performing on schedule or at the estimated costs.

cost/schedule control system criteria (C/SCSC)
(1) Performance measurement approach, with earned value as the primary point of focus.
(2) Criteria that specify the minimum requirements that a contractor's management control system must satisfy.

cost/schedule status report (C/SSR)
Information submitted by U.S. federal government contractors on contracts that are not of sufficient size to warrant a cost performance report, which is generally required with a funding level of at least US$2 million and a contract period in excess of 12 months. The C/SSR, which contains a summary

form, brief narrative on status, and problem analysis report if thresholds are exceeded, is intended to provide the project manager with a description of the contract's cost and schedule status at a given time.

cost/time slope
Theoretical continuum identifying the incremental unit cost required to reduce activity duration by a specific time period.

cost-benefit analysis
See benefit-cost analysis.

cost-effective
Best value or performance for the least cost.

cost-plus-award fee (CPAF) contract
Cost-reimbursement contract that provides for a fee that consists of (1) a base fee (which may be zero) fixed at inception of the contract and (2) an award fee based on a periodic judgmental evaluation by the procuring authority. Used to provide motivation for performance in areas such as quality, timeliness, technical ingenuity, and cost-effective management during the contract. In cost type contracts, the performance risk is borne mostly by the buyer, not the seller.

cost-plus-fixed fee (CPFF) contract
Type of contract in which the buyer reimburses the contractor for the contractor's allowable costs (as defined by the contract) plus a fixed amount of profit (fee). The fixed fee does not vary with actual cost but may be adjusted if changes occur in the work to be performed under the contract. In cost type contracts, the performance risk is borne mostly by the buyer, not the seller.

cost-plus-incentive fee (CPIF) contract
Type of contract in which the buyer reimburses the contractor for the contractor's allowable costs (as defined by the contract) and the seller earns its fee (profit) if it meets defined performance or cost criteria. Specifies a target cost, target fee, minimum fee, maximum fee, and fee adjustment formula.

After contract performance, the fee (profit) paid to the contractor is determined according to the formula.

cost-plus-percentage-of-cost (CPPC) contract
Type of contract that provides reimbursement of allowable cost of services performed plus an agreed-upon percentage of the estimated cost as profit. In cost type contracts, the performance risk is borne mostly by the buyer, not the seller.

cost-reimbursement contract
Contract category that involves payment (reimbursement) to the contractor for its actual costs.

cost-sharing contract
Arrangement under which the contractor bears some of the burden of reasonable, allocable, and allowable contract cost.

cost-time profiles
Graphical illustration depicting accumulated cost against accumulated time. Have been used in conjunction with just-in-time manufacturing, business process reengineering, and total quality management.

CPAF
See cost-plus-award fee contract.

CPFF
See cost-plus-fixed fee contract.

CPI
See cost performance index.

CPIF
See cost-plus-incentive fee contract.

CPM
See critical path method.

CPN
See critical path network.

CPPC

See cost-plus-percentage-of-cost contract.

CPR

See cost performance report.

crashing

Taking action to decrease the total project duration by adding resources (human and material) to the project schedule without altering the sequence of activities. The objective of crashing is to obtain the maximum duration compression for the least cost. *See also* duration compression.

criteria

Objectives, guidelines, procedures, and standards to be used for project development, design, or implementation.

critical activity

Activity on a critical path, commonly determined by using the critical path method.

critical chain

Name of a book by Eliyahu M. Goldratt, as well as the term used to describe the two constraints affecting any project: the critical path and the scarce resources that need to be managed. To keep the critical chain flowing smoothly, Goldratt advises project managers to use safety buffers to allow extra time for tasks that impinge directly on the critical path.

critical defect

Defect that judgment and experience indicate is likely to result in hazardous or unsafe conditions for individuals using, maintaining, or depending on the product or that is likely to prevent performance of the tactical function of the product.

critical defective

Unit of product that contains one or more critical defects and may also contain major or minor defects.

critical issue

Aspect of a system's capability (operational, technical, or other) that must be investigated before the system's overall suitability can be known. Must be addressed before deciding whether to proceed to the next phase of development.

critical item

(1) Subsystem, component, material, or other item whose nonavailability when required could jeopardize completion of project objectives.

(2) Item that could have an adverse impact on cost, schedule, quality, or technical performance.

critical path

In a project network diagram, the series of activities that determine the earliest completion of the project. Will change as activities are completed ahead of or behind schedule. Although normally calculated for the entire project, may also be determined for a milestone or subproject. Often defined as those activities with float less than or equal to a specified value, often zero. *See also* critical path method.

critical path method (CPM)

Network analysis technique used to predict project duration by analyzing the sequence of activities (path) that has the least amount of scheduling flexibility (the least amount of float). Early dates are calculated by a forward pass using a specified start date. Late dates are calculated by a backward pass starting from a specified completion date (usually the forward pass's calculated early finish date for the project).

critical path network (CPN)

Project plan consisting of activities and their logical relationships to one another. Output of the critical path method.

critical risk

Risk that can jeopardize achievement of a project's cost, time, or performance objectives.

culture
In project management, the combined effect of the values, beliefs, attitudes, traditions, and behaviors of the members of an organization.

cumulative cost curve
Graphic display used to show planned and actual expenditures to monitor cost variances. The difference in height between the curves for planned expenditures and actual expenditures represents the monetary value of spending variance at any given time.

current costs
Present market value of a product, asset, or service.

current finish date
Current estimate of the point in time when an activity will finish.

current liabilities
Debts incurred by a corporation, which are expected to be paid within the following 12 months.

current start date
Current estimate of the point in time when an activity will begin.

customer
See client.

customer acceptance
Documented signoff by the customer that all project deliverables satisfy requirements.

customer/client personnel
Individuals working for the organization that will assume responsibility for the product produced by the project when the project is complete.

cutoff point

Minimum acceptable rate of return a corporation is willing to earn on its investments. Often used as one criteria in project selection. *See also* hurdle rate.

cutover

Process of moving from one system to another. Generally refers to a method in which no parallel use of the two systems occurs, making the cutover process a high-risk event should the target system fail to work properly the first time.

CV

See cost variance.

CWBS

See contract work breakdown structure.

cybernetic control system

Automatic control system containing a negative feedback loop.

cycle-time reduction

Any activity that reduces the time it takes an organization to produce a product or deliver a service by minimizing waiting time, eliminating activities that do not add value, increasing parallel processes, or speeding up the decision processes within an organization.

D

damages

Pecuniary compensation or indemnity that may be recovered in a judicial or quasi-judicial forum by a party who suffers loss, detriment, or injury through breach of contract by the act, omission, or negligence of another party.

data

Documented information, regardless of its form or the media on which it is recorded.

data collection
 Gathering and recording of facts, changes, and forecasts for
 status reporting and future planning.

data date
 Point in time that separates actual (historical) data from future
 (scheduled) data. *Also called* as-of date.

data refinement
 Necessary rework or redefinition of logic or data developed
 during planning to properly input milestones, constraints,
 priorities, and resources.

date of acceptance
 Date on which customer provides final approval of the
 deliverable item or project. Commitments against the capital
 authorization cease at that time.

DCF
 See discounted cash flow.

de facto authority
 Influence exercised regardless of formal authority and often
 derived from such power bases as charisma, expert knowledge,
 position, or bureaucratic knowledge. May be exercised by the
 project manager or by project team members. *See also* de jure
 authority.

de jure authority
 Influence based on conferment of the "legal" or rightful power
 to command or act. Usually, the formal authority of a project
 manager is described in some form of documentation (such as
 a project charter), which may also describe the roles of other
 functional managers associated with the project. *See also* de
 facto authority.

decentralized contracting
 Contract management structure in which the project manager
 typically has control over the contracting process for his or her
 project. Either the project manager or a person working

directly for the project manager is responsible for contracting activities.

decision making

Analyzing a problem to identify viable solutions and then making a choice among them.

decision support system

Computer software used to aid in decision making. Simulation programs, mathematical programming routines, and decision rules may be involved.

decision theory

Technique used in risk quantification to assist in decision making, which points to the best possible course of action, considering project uncertainties.

decision tree

Diagram that shows key interactions among decisions and associated chance events as they are understood by the decision maker. Branches of the tree represent either decisions or chance events. The diagram provides for the consideration of the probability of each outcome.

decomposition

Subdivision of the major project deliverables into smaller, more manageable components until the deliverables are defined in sufficient detail to support future project activities (planning, executing, controlling, and closing).

decrement

Cost or price reduction.

default

Failure to perform a legal or contractual duty, honor a promise, discharge an obligation, or perform according to an agreement.

defect

Nonconformance of a characteristic with specified requirements, or a deficiency in something necessary for an item's intended, proper use.

defective
Unit of product that contains one or more defects.

defective cost or pricing data
Cost or pricing data subsequently found to have been inaccurate, incomplete, or not current.

defects per hundred units
Number of defects per hundred units of any given quantity of product, determined by multiplying the number of defects by 100 and then dividing by the total number of units of product. Expressed as an equation: Defects per 100 units = (Number of defects $\times$ 100) $\div$ Number of units.

definitive estimate
Detailed estimate that is prepared from well-defined data, specifications, or drawings and accurate to within -5 to $+10$ percent. Used for bid proposals, bid evaluations, contract changes, legal claims, permits, and government approvals.

deflection
Transference of all or part of a risk to another party, usually by means of a contract provision, insurance policy, or warranty.

delegating
Process of distributing authority from the project manager to another individual working on the project.

deliverable
Measurable, tangible, verifiable outcome, result, or item that must be produced to complete a project or part of a project. Often used more narrowly in reference to an external deliverable, which is a deliverable that is subject to approval by the project sponsor or customer.

Delphi technique
Form of participative expert judgment; an iterative, anonymous, interactive technique using survey methods to derive consensus on work estimates, approaches, and issues.

Deming cycle

See plan-do-check-act (PDCA) cycle.

Deming Prize

Established in Japan in 1951 by the Union of Japanese Scientists and Engineers and named after the father of the worldwide quality movement, W. Edwards Deming. The award honors Japanese and non-Japanese private and public organizations for successfully implementing quality control activities. Evaluation criteria for the award consists of the following 10 equally weighted areas: policies, organization, information standardization, human resources, quality assurance, maintenance, improvement, effects, and future plans.

democratic management style

Participative management approach in which the project manager and project team make decisions jointly.

demonstration

Verifying compliance with the specifications by witnessing how something works or operates.

dependability technique

Method of analyzing a system's behavior, starting at the design level, to identify improvements resulting in increased reliability.

dependency

Logical relationship between and among tasks of a project's WBS, which can be graphically depicted on a network diagram. *See also* logical relationship.

dependent tasks

Tasks that are related such that the beginning or end of one task is contingent on the beginning or end of another.

depreciation

Charge to current operations that systematically and logically distributes the cost of a tangible capital asset less residual value over the asset's estimated useful life.

design

Creation of the description of a product or service, in the form of specifications, drawings, data flow diagrams, or any other methods, to provide detailed information on how to build the product or perform the service.

design of experiments

Analytical technique used in quality management to help identify the variables that have the most influence on the outcome of a process or procedure.

design review

Formal, documented, comprehensive, and systematic examination of a design to evaluate its capability to meet specified requirements, identify problems, and propose solutions.

design specification

Precise measurements, tolerances, materials, in-process and finished-product tests, quality control measures, inspection requirements, and other specific information that precisely describes how the work is to be done.

design to cost

Management concept stipulating that (1) rigorous cost goals are established during the development of a system and (2) control of costs, acquisition, operations, and support is achieved by practical trade-offs between operational capability, performance, costs, and schedule.

design/build

Method of construction contracting that combines the architectural, engineering, and construction services required for a project into a single agreement. Under such an agreement, the buyer contracts with a single entity, so that the contractor providing the end product is responsible for both design and construction.

detailed design

Output of system design; a technical or engineering description of a system that provides individual views of the system components; details on the physical layout of the system; and information on the system's individual applications, subsystems, and hardware components.

detailed schedule

Schedule used to communicate the day-to-day activities to the people working on the project.

deterministic estimate

Predetermined estimate with no possibility of an alternative outcome.

development methodology

Set of mutually supportive and integrated processes and procedures organized into a series of phases constituting the development cycle of a product or service.

development phase

Second of four sequential phases in the generic project life cycle, where project planning and design typically occur. *Also called* planning phase.

deviation

(1) Departure from established requirements.
(2) Written authorization, granted before manufacture of an item, to depart from a specific performance or design requirement.

deviation permit

See production permit.

differentiation in organization

Principle of bureaucratic organization, which states that an organization should be structured around the environment with which it interacts. For example, if a company deals with petroleum interests, it might form a Petroleum Department, further subdivided by types or sources of petroleum.

direct cost

Cost identified with a specific, final cost objective. Not necessarily limited to items that are incorporated into the end product as labor or material. *See also* indirect cost.

direct labor

Labor identified with a specific, final cost objective. For example, manufacturing direct labor includes fabrication, assembly, inspection, and test for constructing the end product; engineering direct labor includes reliability, quality assurance, test, and design identified with the end product. Direct labor is incurred for the exclusive benefit of the project.

direct materials

Raw materials, purchased parts, interdivisional transfers, and subcontracted items required to manufacture and assemble completed products.

direct overhead

Portion of overhead costs that can be directly attributable to a project, such as rent, lighting, and insurance.

direct project costs

Costs directly attributable to a project, including all personnel, goods, or services and their associated costs, but not including indirect project costs, such as overhead and general office costs incurred in support of the project.

directive

Written communication that initiates or prescribes action, conduct, or procedure.

disallowance

Refusal to recognize a cost as an allowable cost.

discipline

Area of technical expertise or specialty.

discount rate

Interest rate used in calculating the present value of future cash flow. *See also* discounted cash flow.

discounted cash flow (DCF)
Financial technique for calculating the present value of future expected expenditures and revenues using net present value.

discrete work package
Short-term, measurable job with a definite start and end point that can be used to measure work performance or earned value.

discretionary dependency
Dependency defined by preference, rather than necessity. *Also called* preferred logic, preferential logic, *or* soft logic.

dispute
(1) Disagreement not settled by mutual consent that could be decided by litigation or arbitration.
(2) Disagreement between the contractor and the buyer regarding the rights of parties under a contract.

disruptive management style
Management approach in which the project manager tends to destroy the unity of the team, be an agitator, and cause disorder on the project.

distance learning
Method of providing education and training to an individual or group of individuals in which the learner(s) is not in the same room as the provider (teacher, professor, instructor) of the information. Requires the use of one or more of a variety of techniques and media to present the subject matter and can include television, satellite broadcasts, correspondence, e-mail, computer-based training, CD ROM, videotape, Web-based delivery, or any combination thereof. Distance learning is viewed by many executives as a way to slash training costs by eliminating the need for employees to travel to a course site, as well as having them complete all or part of the training on their own time.

division of labor

Specifically assigning persons to various activities within a project by categories of labor, skill, or expertise.

document control

System to control and execute project documentation in a uniform and orderly fashion.

documentation

Collection of reports, information, records, references, and other project data for distribution and archival purposes.

DU

See duration.

dummy activity

Activity of zero duration that shows a logical relationship in the arrow diagramming method. Used when logical relationships cannot be completely or correctly described with regular activity arrows. Shown graphically as a dashed line headed by an arrow.

duration (DU)

Number of work periods required to complete an activity or other project element. Usually expressed as hours, workdays, or workweeks. Sometimes incorrectly equated with elapsed time. *See also* effort.

duration compression

Shortening of the schedule without reducing the project scope. Often requires an increase in project cost. *Also called* schedule compression. *See also* crashing *and* fast-tracking.

E

EAC

See estimate at completion.

early finish date (EF)

Earliest possible point in time when the uncompleted portions of an activity (or the project) can end based on network logic and any schedule constraints. May change as the project progresses or as changes are made to the project plan. Used in the critical path method.

early start date (ES)

Earliest possible point in time when the uncompleted portions of an activity (or the project) can begin, based on network logic and any schedule constraints. May change as the project progresses or as changes are made to the project plan. Used in the critical path method.

early warning system

Project control monitoring and reporting system used to alert the project manager if trouble is about to arise.

earned hours

Time in standard hours credited to a worker or group of workers as the result of successfully completing a given task or group of tasks; usually calculated by summing the products of applicable standard times multiplied by the completed work units.

earned value (EV)

Analysis of a project's schedule and financial progress as compared to the original plan. *See also* actual cost of work performed, budgeted cost of work scheduled, budgeted cost of work performed, budget at completion, cost variance, cost performance index, schedule variance, *and* schedule performance index.

earned value analysis

See earned value.

earned value systems

Technique, procedure, or approach that uses the earned value method of information collection and reporting for a project or program. Can be completed manually or using information technology. *See also* earned value.

e-business (electronic business)
Conducting all facets of business on the Internet. Applications include, and go beyond, the types of commercial transactions commonly conducted in e-commerce, such as customer relationship management and partner collaboration. Term is used by certain organizations in their advertising campaigns to generally describe a range of service offerings as they relate to conducting business over the Internet.

e-commerce (electronic commerce)
Conducting business transactions between businesses, or between businesses and consumers usually over the Web, or by other automated means. Popular applications of e-commerce include the following on-line activities: buying products; paying bills; conducting banking activities; and booking airline, car, and hotel reservations.

economic analysis phase
See concept phase.

economic evaluation
Process used to establish the value of a project in relation to other standards, benchmarks, project profitability, financing interest rates, and acceptance.

economic lot size
Number of units of manufactured items or materials that can be purchased within the lowest unit cost range.

economic value added (EVA)
Nonconventional accounting practice that measures an operation's real profitability. EVA is simply after-tax operating profit, a widely used measure, minus the total annual cost of capital, which no conventional measure includes.

economy of scale
Reduction in the unit cost of an end product resulting from the production of additional units.

EF
See early finish date.

effective interest
True value of the interest rate computed using equations for compound interest rate for a 1-year period.

effective team
Group of people who work with each other in a positive way to accomplish shared objectives.

efficiency factor
Ratio of standard performance time to actual performance, usually expressed as a percentage.

effort
Number of labor units required to complete an activity or other project element. May be expressed as staff hours, days, or weeks. Should not be confused with duration.

egoless team structure
Way of organizing a project team in which there is no obvious leader, decisions are reached through consensus, and project tasks tend to reflect the input of all team members. Promotes extensive interaction and communication but, without strong consensual leadership, the team can drift. Works best when the team is small, objectives are clear, and the task being accomplished is of high importance.

eighty-hour rule
Method of breaking down each project activity or task into work packages that require no more than 80 hours of effort to complete.

elaborated
Worked out with care and detail; developed thoroughly.

elapsed time
Conventional concept of time with a 60-minute hour and 365-day year. Accounts for all time, not just time spent on the project.

e-learning (electronic learning)
Form of distance learning that is Internet based.

employee stock ownership plans (ESOP)
Under an ESOP, employees take over, or participate in, the management of the organization that employs them by becoming shareholders of stock in that organization.

end product
Deliverable resulting from project work.

end user
Person or group for whom the project's product or service is developed.

endorsement
Written approval that signifies personal understanding and acceptance of the thing approved and recommends further endorsement by higher levels of authority if necessary; signifies authorization if endorsement of commitment is by a person with appropriate authority.

engineering build-up estimate
See bottom-up estimate.

engineering change notice
Formal release of an engineering change to the performing organizations.

engineering change order
Directive to incorporate project improvements that have been designed after release of the initial product design.

engineering change proposal
Request initiated by either party to make changes to the drawings or specifications of a contract.

engineering estimate
See definitive estimate.

engineering review board (ERB)

Committee of senior personnel from the functional engineering organizations convened to provide technical oversight for, and assistance to, the project manager. Usually convened at the request of the project manager. Members are appointed by the director of engineering or by the director's designee.

enhancement

Change or group of changes to the scope of an existing project that provides additional functionality, features, or capabilities.

enterprise

(1) Company or organization.
(2) Subpart of a company or organization.
(3) Business of a customer.

enterprise model

Approach used to describe aspects of a business or organization, including mission, goals, objectives, processes, information requirements, and business activities.

enterprise project management (EPM)

Comprehensive implementation and practice of project management based on the recognition that the sum total of an organization's work is a portfolio of simultaneous and interconnected projects that need to be managed collectively as well as individually. EPM is brought about by the consistent efforts of the project office—or other organizational entity—to support project managers throughout the organization. Organizations that implement EPM generally regard project management as a key competency and, therefore, develop education and training programs, career paths, and associated reward systems to firmly establish project management as a professional discipline with its own identity. Additionally, such organizations facilitate the consistent application of project management practices through the deployment of a methodology as well as by providing on-the-job support through a program management office or center of excellence. *See also* project office.

environment

(1) Aggregate of all cultural, political, geographical, physical, and technical conditions surrounding and influencing a project.
(2) Boundaries of a business area.

EPM

See enterprise project management

equipment

Machines, tools, or other hardware items necessary to complete a project or task.

equipment procurement

Acquisition of equipment or material to be used in the project.

equitable adjustment

Fair price adjustment under a contract clause for changed work, including an adjustment in profit; a change in the delivery schedule, if appropriate; and a change in any other affected terms of the contract.

equivalent units

Approach used to determine the budget and calculate earned value and in which a given value is placed on each unit completed. Applies best to manufacturing efforts.

ERB

See engineering review board.

ES

See early start date.

escalation

Conversion of past to present prices or present to future prices through use of a price index.

e-signature (electronic signature)

Electronic sound, symbol, or process, attached to or logically associated with a contract or other record and executed or adopted by a person with the intent to sign the record. Can be a typed name a person attaches to an e-mail message or a digitized image of a signature that is associated with a special algorithm that verifies the authenticity of the electronic document. In the United States, the Electronic Signatures in Global and National Commerce Act, signed into law in June 2000, governs the use of e-signatures. Speeds the contracting process and makes it easier for businesses to conduct e-commerce as well as more traditional forms of commerce.

estimate

Assessment of likely quantitative result, usually applied to project costs and durations. Should include some indication of accuracy (for example, ± X percent). Generally used with a modifier (such as preliminary, conceptual, or feasibility). Some disciplines use modifiers that imply specific accuracy ranges (such as order-of-magnitude, budget, and definitive, which have been traditionally used in engineering and construction projects), but are increasingly used in other industry applications.

estimate at completion (EAC)

Expected total cost of an activity, group of activities, or total project when the work is complete. Forecast of total project costs based on project performance to date. PMBOK® provides three methods of calculating EAC: EAC=ACWP+ETC; BAC÷CPI; and ACWP+BCWS. *Also called* forecast at completion *or* latest revised estimate. *See also* earned value *and* estimate to complete.

estimate to complete (ETC)

Expected additional cost needed to complete an activity, group of activities, or the total project. Most techniques for forecasting ETC include an adjustment to the original estimate based on project performance to date. *See also* earned value *and* estimate at completion.

estimated cost

Anticipated cost of performance of a project.

estimated final cost
Anticipated cost of a completed project or component. Sum of the committed cost to date and the estimated cost to complete. *Also called* forecast final cost. *See also* estimate at completion.

estimating
Forecasting the cost, schedule, and resource requirements needed to produce a specific deliverable.

estimating guidelines
Procedures for estimating project work effort, cost, or schedule, including formulas and criteria for assessing the major factors affecting the cost estimate.

ETC
See estimate to complete.

ethical management style
Management approach in which the project manager is honest, sincere, and able to motivate and press for the best and fairest solution.

e-training (electronic training)
See e-learning.

European Foundation for Quality Management (EFQM) Excellence Model
Nonprescriptive framework based on nine criteria and 32 subcriteria used to assess an organization's progress towards business excellence. Based on the premise that customer satisfaction, people satisfaction, and impact on society are achieved through excellence that focuses on policy and strategy, people management, resources, and processes.

European quality award
Award established and presented by the European Foundation for Quality Management (EFQM) to those European firms that demonstrate commitment to business excellence in accordance with the EFQM Excellence Model. *See also* European Foundation for Quality Management Excellence Model.

EV

See earned value.

EVA

See economic value added.

evaluate

Appraise against a set value.

evaluation criteria

Rationale used to weight or score proposals submitted by prospective contractors; may be either objective or subjective.

event

(1) Activity that does not use resources; a milestone.

(2) End state for one or more activities that occur at a specific point in time. Used to show a critical point in a project, such as a decision point or the start or completion of a task or group of tasks.

(3) Significant occurrence that obligates the organization to take action.

(4) Key component of risk. Usually a description of the negative or positive incident associated with a risk.

event chart

See milestone chart.

event-on-node

Network diagramming technique in which events are represented by boxes (or nodes) connected by arrows to show the sequence in which the events are to occur. Used in the Program Evaluation and Review Technique.

examination

Element of inspection consisting of investigation of supplies and services to determine conformance to specified requirements without using special laboratory equipment or procedures.

exception report

Document that includes only significant variances from the project baselines (rather than all variances). *See also* significant variance.

exception reporting

Process of documenting those situations where significant variances from project specifications (baselines) have occurred. *See also* significant variance.

executed contract

Signed, consummated contract, the terms and conditions of which have been completely fulfilled by the parties.

executing processes

Activities associated with coordinating people and other resources to implement the project plan.

execution phase

See implementation phase.

expectancy theory

Theory of motivation, which holds that people will tend to be highly motivated and productive if they believe that (1) their efforts will likely lead to successful results and (2) they will be rewarded for their success.

expectations

Anticipated changes in performance as a result of project implementation. May be in the areas of business, productivity, operations, culture, and others.

expected monetary value

Product of an event's probability of occurrence and the gain or loss that will result. For example, if there is a 50 percent probability of snow, and snow will result in a $100 loss, the expected monetary value of the snow is $50 ($0.5 \times \$100$).

expected time

Statistically calculated time estimate used in PERT estimating to determine the number of work periods an activity will consume. *See also* probabilistic estimating.

expected value

In risk management, result of multiplying the probability of a variable's occurrence with its estimated monetary impact. Although a theoretical figure, it provides some sense of the value of the loss incurred should the risk occur.

expenditure

Activity or event involving a conversion of resources in the form of (1) an exchange—a conversion of title or ownership (such as money for materials), or (2) a consumption—a conversion of a liquid resource to a less recoverable state (such as an expenditure of time, human resources, or money to produce something of value, or the conversion of inventoried materials to fixed assets).

experience curve

See learning curve.

expert authority

Influence derived from an individual's knowledge or expertise, rather than from some outside source. *Also called* technical authority.

expert judgment

Opinions, advice, recommendations, or commentary proffered, usually upon request, by a person or persons recognized, either formally or informally, as having specialized knowledge or training in a specific area.

expert power

See expert authority.

expert system

Computer software that uses the knowledge of recognized experts in an area and makes inferences about a problem based on decision rules and data input to the software.

exploratory forecasting
Forecasting method that extrapolates from past experience and looks toward the future; used in gap analysis to estimate future budget demands of projects in a portfolio.

express warranty
Promise actually spoken or written in an agreement.

external audit
Audit performed by anyone outside the project team.

external dependency
Dependency that involves a relationship between project and nonproject activities.

external feedback
Evaluative information about the performance of the project team from individuals outside the project and, typically, outside the organization.

external risk
Risk beyond the control or influence of the project team. *See also* internal risk.

F

FAC
See forecast at completion.

facilitating management style
Management approach in which the project manager makes himself or herself available to answer questions and provide guidance when needed but does not interfere with day-to-day tasks.

facilitator
Person external to a group whose purpose is to help the group work more effectively.

facilities capital

Net book value of tangible and intangible capital assets subject to amortization.

facilities contract

Contract under which the buyer provides work space, equipment, tools, and so on to a contractor or subcontractor for use in performing one or more related contracts for supplies and services.

failure modes and effect analysis (FMEA)

Analysis process that examines various ways in which a product or service may fail and the effect of those failures on the system. Using FMEA, a project team can identify the most important possible failure modes so that action can be taken to reduce the risk of failure.

fair and reasonable price

Price considered to be fair to both parties based on agreed-upon conditions, promised quality, and timeliness of contract performance.

fair market price

Price at which bona fide sales have been made for assets of like type, quality, and quantity in a particular market at the time of acquisition.

FAS

See free alongside ship.

fast decision process

Process in which a small, empowered, cross-functional or cross-organizational team, with the help of a trained facilitator, makes decisions quickly. Differs from other processes because it concentrates on producing deliverables.

fast-tracking

Compressing the project schedule by overlapping activities normally performed in sequence, such as design and construction. Sometimes confused with concurrent engineering.

fault tolerance

Method used to make a computer or network system resistant to software errors and hardware malfunctions.

fault tree

Diagram that shows the logical combination of causes leading to a particular failure. Because the cause and effect sequences are not limited, a precise analysis can be conducted.

FBS

See functional breakdown structure.

feasibility

Assessment of the capability for successful implementation; the possibility, probability, and suitability of accomplishment.

feasibility estimate

See order-of-magnitude estimate.

feasibility phase

See concept phase.

feasibility study

Examination of technical and cost data to determine the economic potential and practicality of project applications. Involves the use of techniques such as the time value of money so that projects may be evaluated and compared on an equivalent basis. Interest rates, present value factors, capitalization costs, operating costs, and depreciation are all considered.

fee

Amount paid to the contractor beyond its costs under a cost-reimbursement contract. In U.S. federal government procurement, "fee" is the term for the profit the government agrees to pay on a cost-reimbursement contract, and in most cases, the amount of fee reflects a variety of factors, including risk.

fee for professional services

Amount paid under contract for professional and consultant services when the work is performed satisfactorily.

feedback

Information extracted from a process or situation and used to control, plan, or modify immediate or future input to the process or situation.

FF

See finish-to-finish.

FFP

See firm-fixed-price contract.

field cost

Cost associated with establishing, operating, and maintaining the project site rather than the corporate office.

fifty-fifty method of progress reporting

Method used in earned value analysis to estimate the amount of each task that has been completed. As soon as a task has started, half the effort is assumed to be completed and half the BCWS value associated with the task is entered into the project accounts book. Only after the task is actually completed is the remaining half of the BCWS value entered into the accounts. This approach provides a good statistical approximation of the BCWP for the project when there are many tasks under way of approximately the same magnitude.

filtering

Selectively screening the thoughts and ideas of the communicator according to one's own frame of reference, attitudes, beliefs, expectations, and relationship to the communicator.

final completion

Certification that the entire work has been performed to the requirements of the contract, except for those items arising from the provisions of warranty.

final payment
Final settlement, paid at contract completion, of the contractually obligated amount including any retention.

final system design
Full-scale, approved product design prepared from customer requirements and the initial system design.

financial closeout
Accounting analysis of how funds were spent on the project. Signifies a point in time when no further charges should be made against the project.

financial control
See cost control.

financial statement
Written record listing the financial status of an individual or organization, including assets and liabilities.

financing
Raising funds required for the project using techniques and methods such as stocks, mortgages, bonds, innovative financing agreements, or leases.

finish date
Point in time associated with an activity's or project's completion. Usually qualified by terms such as actual, planned, estimated, scheduled, early, late, baseline, target, or current.

finish-to-finish (FF)
Relationship in a precedence diagramming method network in which one activity must end before the successor activity can end. *See also* logical relationship.

finish-to-start (FS)
Relationship in a precedence diagramming method network in which one activity must end before the successor activity can start. The most commonly used relationship in the precedence diagramming method. *See also* logical relationship.

firm offer

Offer from a seller to a buyer, usually in writing, that is valid for a set period of time.

firm-fixed-price (FFP) contract

Type of contract in which the buyer pays the contractor a set amount (as defined by the contract) regardless of the contractor's costs. In fixed-price contracts, the performance risk is borne mostly by the seller, not the buyer.

FIRO-B awareness scale

Test used to determine how people fit into a group according to three dimensions: inclusion, control, and affection.

first-article testing

Evaluating the first items produced before or in the initial stage of production to see whether they conform with specified contract requirements.

fishbone diagram

See Ishikawa diagram.

fit

Externally imposed constraint for which a project deliverable may have to adapt or conform.

fixed asset

Property or equipment, such as machines, buildings, and land, used for the production of goods and services.

fixed cost

Cost that does not vary with volume of output.

fixed-price contract

Type of contract with a firm pricing arrangement established by the parties at the time of contracting. A firm-fixed-price contract is not subject to adjustment on the basis of the contractor's cost experience in performing the contract. Other types of fixed-price contracts (fixed-price contract with economic price adjustment, fixed-price incentive contract, fixed-priced redetermination prospective contract, and fixed-price redetermination retroactive contract) are subject to price adjustment on the basis of (1) economic conditions or (2) the contractor's performance of the contract.

fixed-price incentive (FPI) contract

Type of contract in which the buyer pays the contractor for the actual allowable cost incurred, not to exceed a ceiling price defined in the contract, and the contractor can earn more or less profit depending on its ability to meet defined performance or cost criteria. In fixed-price contracts, the performance risk is borne mostly by the seller, not the buyer.

fixed-price level-of-effort contract

Type of firm-fixed-price contract requiring the contractor to provide a specified level of effort over a stated period of time on work that can be stated only in general terms.

float

Amount of time that an activity may be delayed from its early start without delaying the project end date. Derived by subtracting the early start from the late start or early finish from the late finish, and may change as the project progresses and as changes are made to the project plan. *Also called* slack, total float, *and* path float. *See also* free float.

floating task

Task that can be performed earlier or later in the schedule without affecting the project duration or critical path.

flow diagram

Graphic representation of work flow and the logical sequence of the work elements without regard to a time scale. Used to show the logic associated with a process rather than a duration for completion of work.

flowchart

Diagram consisting of symbols depicting a physical process, a thought process, or an algorithm. Shows how the various elements of a system or process relate and which can be used for continuous process improvement.

flow-down clauses

Clauses prescribed by the buyer that a prime contractor incorporates into any subcontracts.

FMEA

See failure modes and effect analysis.

FOB

See free on board.

fog index

Method developed by Robert Gunning to measure the readability of a written work (in the English language) based on a combination of two criteria: (1) the average number of words per sentence and (2) the percentage of words containing three or more syllables.

follower

Task that logically succeeds a particular task in time.

follow-up audit

Audit conducted to determine whether the recommendations resulting from a previous audit were implemented and were effective in correcting or preventing the problems noted. Can be either a full or partial audit.

force-field analysis

Quality technique that identifies the various pressures promoting or resisting change.

forcing

See conflict resolution.

forecast

Estimate or prediction of future conditions and events based on information and knowledge available at the time of the estimate.

forecast at completion (FAC)

See estimate at completion.

forecast final cost
See estimated final cost.

forecasting
Estimating or predicting future conditions and events. Generally done during the planning process. Often confused with budgeting, which is a definitive allocation of resources rather than a prediction or estimate.

foreign currency translation
Process of expressing amounts denominated in one currency into terms of a second currency.

foreign exchange
Instruments such as paper currency, notes, checks, and bills of exchange employed in making payments between countries.

formal acceptance
Documentation signifying that the customer or sponsor has accepted the product of the project or phase. May be conditional if the acceptance is for a phase of the project.

formal authority
Influence based on an individual's position in the organization and conferred upon that person by the organization. *Also called* legitimate authority.

formative quality evaluation
Ongoing evaluation process to ensure that project results conform with pre-established quality standards.

formula estimating
Method of work effort estimation using a prescribed method or formula to list and quantify major factors that impact project or product development.

forward pass
Calculation of the early start and early finish dates for the uncompleted portions of all network activities. *See also* network analysis *and* backward pass.

forward pricing

Using progressively escalated labor rates to convert direct labor hours to direct labor monetary values and using progressively escalated overhead rates, direct material, and subcontract monetary values to develop an escalated price estimate. *See also* negotiated bidding rates.

forward scheduling

Method in which the project start date is fixed and task duration and dependency information is used to compute the corresponding project completion date.

FPI

See fixed-price incentive contract.

fragnet

See subnet.

free alongside ship (FAS)

Pricing scheme in which the seller agrees to pay for the shipment of goods from factory to pier.

free float

Amount of time that an activity may be delayed without delaying the early start of any immediately succeeding activities. *Also called* secondary float.

free on board (FOB)

Pricing scheme in which the seller agrees to pay for the shipment of goods to a specific point and no farther.

FS

See finish-to-start.

full and open competition

Method in U.S. federal government procurement in which all responsible sources are permitted to compete for a contract.

full audit

Audit that includes all elements of the project.

functional baseline

Initial approved functional configuration identification. *See also* functional configuration identification.

functional breakdown structure (FBS)

Hierarchical structure relating the function of a product or service. Used in value analysis techniques.

functional configuration identification

Current, approved technical documentation for a configuration item (CI), which prescribes (1) all the necessary functional characteristics; (2) the tests required to demonstrate achievement of specified functional characteristics; (3) the necessary interface characteristics associated with the CI, its key functional characteristics, and its lower-level CIs, if any; and (4) the design constraints.

functional department

Specialized department within an organization that performs a particular function, such as engineering, manufacturing, or marketing.

functional manager

See line manager.

functional organization

Organizational structure in which staff are grouped hierarchically by specialty, such as production, marketing, engineering, and accounting at the top level, with each area further divided into subareas. (For example, engineering can be subdivided into mechanical, electrical, and so on). Coordination is accomplished by functional "line" managers and upper levels of management.

functional organization expert

Customer-provided or internal personnel who are process and knowledge experts, provide validation, and work on technical aspects of the project.

functional requirements

Characteristics of the deliverable described in ordinary, nontechnical language that is understandable to the customer. Customer plays a major, direct role in their development.

functional specification

Description of work to be performed in terms of the end purpose or results, rather than in terms of the specific procedures, processes, or equipment to be used in the performance of the work. May include a description of the qualitative nature of the end product, and may also include a statement of the minimum essential characteristics the product must exhibit to satisfy its intended use.

function-point analysis

Approach to estimating software costs that involves examining the project's initial high-level requirements statements, identifying specific functions, and estimating total costs based on the number of functions to be performed.

function-quality integration

Process of ensuring that quality plans and programs are integrated, consistent, necessary, and sufficient to permit the project team to achieve defined product quality.

funding

Organizational process by which monetary resources for a project are approved and formally allocated to the project.

G

G&A

See general and administrative expense.

gain sharing

Approach in which an organization shares the benefits of improvements, including profits, with its employees. Handled through such mechanisms as suggestion awards paid directly to individuals; employee stock ownership plans; and profit sharing, in which all employees receive a percentage of base pay as a bonus.

Gantt chart

Graphic display of schedule-related information. Generally, activities or other project elements are listed down the left side of the chart, dates are shown across the top, and activity durations are displayed against the x and y axes as date-placed horizontal bars. Named after its developer, Henry Gantt.

gap analysis

(1) Examination of the difference between the current state and the desired or optimum state.

(2) Technique to help visualize the budget options available in project portfolios. Uses exploratory and normative forecasting and compares the curve associated with the total budget requirements of existing projects with that of the total anticipated budget for all projects, even those that are not under way. An anticipated gap can be determined and analyzed.

general and administrative (G&A) expense

Management, financial, or other expense incurred by or allocated to an organizational unit for the general management and administration of the organization as a whole.

general management

Broad subject dealing with every aspect of managing an organization whose work is a continuous stream of activities. General management and project management share similar skills.

general provisions

Legal relationships and responsibilities of the parties to the contract, including how the contract will be administered; usually standard for an organization or project.

general requirements

Nontechnical specifications defining the scope of work, payments, procedures, implementation constraints, and other nontechnical requirements concerning the contract.

general sequencing

Overview of the order in which activities are performed.

GERT

See Graphical Evaluation and Review Technique.

go/no-go

(1) Major decision point in the project life cycle.
(2) Measure that allows a manager to decide whether to continue, change, or end an activity or project.
(3) Type of gauge that tells an inspector if an object's dimension is within certain limits.

goal

Basic component for measuring progress in attaining project objectives.

gold-plating

Providing more than the customer or specifications require, and thus spending more time and money than necessary to achieve quality.

government contract quality assurance

Various functions, including inspection, performed by the U.S. federal government to determine whether a contractor has fulfilled the contract obligations pertaining to quality and quantity.

Gozinto chart

Representation of a product that shows how the elements required to build it fit together.

grade

Category or rank given to items that have the same functional use but do not share the same requirements for quality; low quality is always a problem, but low grade may not be.

grapevine

Informal and unofficial communication path within an organization. Grapevine information has been shown to be accurate but usually incomplete.

graph

Display or diagram that shows the relationship between activities; pictorial representation of relative variables. Examples include trend graphs, histograms, control charts, frequency distributions, and scatter diagrams.

Graphical Evaluation and Review Technique (GERT)

Network analysis technique that allows for conditional and probabilistic treatment of logical relationships (for example, some activities may not be performed). *See also* conditional diagramming method.

grass-roots estimate

See bottom-up estimate.

gross profit

Difference between revenue earned and direct costs of goods or services sold.

group communication

Meetings, presentations, negotiations, and other activities conducted by the project manager to convey information to the project team and other stakeholders.

group dynamics

Social interaction of the participants in a group. Can be positive or negative depending on the makeup and personality characteristics of the persons in the group.

groupware

Generic term used to described any software application program that runs on a network and which allows groups of people to work collectively and collaboratively.

guideline
Document that recommends methods and procedures to be used to accomplish an objective.

H

hammock
Group of related activities that is shown as one aggregate activity and reported at a summary level. May or may not have an internal sequence. *See also* subnet.

hanger
Unintended break in a network path. Usually occurs as a result of missing activities or missing logical relationships.

hard copy
Printed information output as contrasted with electronic presentation.

hard logic
See mandatory dependency.

Herzberg's theory of motivation
Theory of motivation developed by Fredrick Herzberg in which he asserts that individuals are affected by two opposing forms of motivation: hygiene factors and motivators. Hygiene factors such as pay, attitude of supervisor, and working conditions serve only to demotivate people if they are not provided in the type or amount required by the person. Improving hygiene factors under normal circumstances is not likely to increase motivation. Factors such as greater freedom, more responsibility, and more recognition serve to enhance self-esteem and are considered the motivators that energize and stimulate the person to enhanced performance.

heuristic
Problem-solving technique that results in an acceptable solution; often arrived at by trial and error.

hidden agenda

Objectives of a person or group of persons not made known to others during the course of a project and which tend to subvert the stated objectives of the project or work contrary to them.

hierarchical management

Traditional functional, or line, management in which areas and subareas of expertise are created and staffed with human resources. Organizations so established are ongoing in nature.

high-performance work teams

Group of people who work together in an interdependent manner such that their collective performance exceeds that which would be achieved by simply adding together their individual contributions. Characteristics of such a team include strong group identity, collaboration, anticipating and acting on other team member needs, and a laser-like focus on project objectives.

histogram

Timeline chart that shows the use of a resource over time.

historic records

Project documentation used to predict trends, analyze feasibility, and highlight possible problem areas or pitfalls on subsequent similar projects.

historical cost

Actual cost incurred in performing the work.

historical estimating

Method of estimating work effort and costs using documented data from past projects or from similar tasks as the major input to the estimating process.

holistic

Oriented toward viewing the whole rather than considering each piece individually.

human resource Gantt chart

Variation of the horizontal bar Gantt chart. Graphically illustrates how personnel resources are allocated, task by task, and how those resources are distributed throughout the life of a project. Used to track and plan personnel allocations and to identify when resources are overallocated.

human resource loading chart

Vertical bar chart used to show personnel resource consumption by time period.

human resource management

See project human resource management.

hurdle rate

In a discounted cash-flow analysis, required rate of return expected from a corporation in order to proceed with a project, product, or new service. *See also* cutoff point.

hygiene factors

According to Frederick Herzberg's Motivator-Hygiene Theory, factors related to job dissatisfaction that must be addressed to retain employees, such as pay, attitude of supervisor, or working conditions. *See also* Motivator-Hygiene Theory.

I

idea phase

See concept phase.

idle time

Time interval during which the project team, equipment, or both, do not perform useful work.

IFB

See invitation for bid.

impact

Estimate of the effect that a risk will have on schedule, costs, product quality, safety, and performance.

impact analysis
Qualitative or quantitative assessment of the magnitude of loss or gain to be realized should a specific risk or opportunity event—or series of interdependent events—occur.

implementation phase
Third of four sequential phases in the generic project life cycle in which the project plan is executed, monitored, and controlled. *Also called* execution *or* operation phase.

implied warranty
Promise that is implicitly included in a transaction regardless of whether it is expressly written. For example, the implied warranty of merchantability states that goods or products must be reasonably fit for the ordinary purposes(s) for which they are used. *See also* express warranty.

imposed date (external)
(1) Predetermined calendar date set without regard to network-logical considerations or resource requirements. (2) Specified date that is required by the project sponsor, the project customer, or other external factors for completion of certain deliverables.

inaccuracy allowance
Allocation of time or money to cover possible inaccuracy in schedule or cost estimates.

incentive contract
Negotiated pricing arrangement that gives the contractor higher profits for better performance or lower profits for worse performance in stated areas (cost, schedule, or technical performance).

incremental approach
Phased approach to project completion whereby certain project functionalities and capabilities are delivered in phases. Allows stakeholders to realize certain benefits earlier than if they were to wait for the total project to be completed.

indefinite-delivery contract
In U.S. federal government procurement, a type of contract in which the period of performance is not specified in the original contract but is established by the contracting officer during performance.

indefinite-quantity contract
In U.S. federal government procurement, a type of contract with an indefinite quantity (within stated minimum or maximum limits) of specific supplies or services to be furnished during a fixed period, with deliveries to be scheduled by placing orders with the contractor.

indemnification
Act of reimbursing a person for a loss already incurred. Two general types exist: common-law and contractual.

independent cost estimate
(1) Estimate of project costs conducted by individuals outside the normal project management structure.
(2) Estimate of anticipated project costs by the project team; used to compare the reasonableness of contractor proposals.

independent verification and validation (IV&V)
Process used to verify and validate software or some other product, by a group other than the one that created or implemented the original design.

indirect cost
(1) Cost not directly identified with one final cost objective. May be identified with two or more final or one or more intermediate cost objectives.
(2) Cost allocated to the project by the performing organization as a cost of doing business. *Also called* overhead cost *or* burden. *See also* direct cost.

indirect cost pool
Group of incurred costs identified with two or more cost objectives but not specifically identified with any final cost objective.

indirect prejudice

Cost that results from a product failure or failure to meet contractual commitments, such as loss of market share for the customer's organization. Can be calculated by average growth compared to reduced growth because of loss of production capability. Generally not covered by insurance.

inflation

Factor in cost evaluation and cost comparison that must be predicted as an allowance for the price changes that occur with time and over which the project manager has no control, such as the cost of living index, interest rates, and other cost indices.

influencing the organization

Ability to "get things done." Requires an understanding of both the formal and informal structures of all the organizations, powers, and politics involved.

information distribution

Timely provision of needed information to project stakeholders in a variety of formats.

information overload

Exposure to such quantity, type, and complexity of information input that one's ability to comprehend, assimilate, and use such information is increasingly diminished.

information requirement

Information needed to perform day-to-day operations.

information system

Complex, interactive structure of people, equipment, processes, and procedures designed to produce information collected from both internal and external sources for use in decision-making activities.

inherently governmental activities

Term used in U.S. government activities. Defines an activity as one that is so intimately related to the public interest that it must be done by federal employees. Normally fall into two categories: (1) the act of governing, that is, the discretionary exercise of government authority, and (2) monetary transactions and entitlements.

in-house

Work performed by one's own employees as opposed to an outside contractor.

initial project plan

(1) Top-down, high-level plan used to document the early approach to a project; usually contains resource manager commitments and a preliminary technical solution.
(2) Method for communication during the delegation of a project responsibility and acceptance of a project commitment.

initiating processes

Procedures for recognizing that a project or phase should begin and committing to start it.

initiation

Process of formally recognizing that a new project exists or that an existing project should continue into its next phase.

in-progress activity

Activity that has started but not been completed as of a given date.

input

(1) Information or other items required to begin a process or activity.
(2) Documents or documentable items to be acted upon.
(3) Information, thoughts, or ideas used to assist in decision making.

input limits

Limitations imposed on the resources needed to execute the plan.

input milestone

Imposed target dates or target events that are to be accomplished and that control the plan with respect to time.

input priorities
Imposed priorities or sequence desired with respect to the scheduling activities within previously imposed constraints.

input restraint
Imposed external constraint, such as dates reflecting input from others, target dates reflecting output required by others, or float allocation.

in-service date
Time when the project's product or service is placed in a state of readiness or availability so that it can be used for its specifically assigned function.

inspection
Examination or measurement of work to verify whether an item or activity conforms to a specific requirement.

inspection by attributes
Inspection in which either the unit of product or characteristics of the product are classified as defective or nondefective or the number of defects in the unit of product is counted with respect to a given requirement.

inspection by variables
Inspection in which certain quality characteristics of the sample are evaluated with respect to a continuous numerical scale and are expressed as precise points along this scale. Records the degree of conformance or nonconformance of the unit with specified requirements for the quality characteristics involved.

inspection cycle
System in which supplies and equipment in storage are subjected to, but not limited to, periodic, special inspection and continuous action to ensure that material is maintained in a ready-for-issue condition.

inspection level
Indication of the relative sample size for a given amount of product.

inspection record
Recorded data concerning the results of inspection action.

inspection system requirement
Requirement to establish and maintain an inspection system according to a directed (for example, government) specification; requirement referenced in contracts when technical requirements necessitate control of quality by in-process and final end-item inspection.

inspection-in-process
Inspection performed during the manufacturing or repair cycle to help prevent defectives from occurring and to inspect the characteristics and attributes that cannot be examined at final inspection.

insurable risk
Risk that can be covered by an insurance policy. *Also called* pure risk.

insurance
(1) Premium paid to a person or organization to cover some or all of the cost of a risk impact. *See also* impact.
(2) Protection against a risk of loss or harm.

integrated cost/schedule reporting
Output of earned value analysis.

integrated logistics support (ILS)
Composite of all considerations necessary to ensure the effective and economical support of a system over its life cycle. Principal elements include—

- Maintenance planning
- Supply support
- Technical data
- Facilities
- Staffing and personnel
- Training and training support
- Support equipment
- Computer resources support

- Packaging, handling, storage, and transportation
- Design interfaces

integrated product development team (IPDT)
Group of people from different functional disciplines whose collective effort is required to complete a given product development project and who meet at frequent and regular intervals to plan, execute, and monitor project performance. Meets at the outset to plan the entire project even though many of its members may not be involved with project execution until many months, or years, after the project begins. It has been shown that this type of team can accelerate project completion because all team members (1) agree on the project's objectives at the beginning of the project; (2) understand their roles, as well as the roles of the others, in project execution; and (3) know the exact time when they are required to work on the project.

integrated project progress report
Documentation that measures actual cost and schedule data against the budget by using BCWP, BCWS, and ACWP.

intellectual property
Concept, idea, notion, thought, or process, including a computer program, that is definable, measurable, and proprietary in nature.

intention to bid
Communication, written or oral, from prospective contractors indicating their willingness to perform the specified work. Could be by a letter, statement of qualifications, or response to a request for proposals or request for quotations.

interdependencies
Relationships among organizational functions in which one function, task, or activity is dependent on others.

interest
Amount paid for the use of money.

interface activity

(1) Activity connecting a node in one subnet with a node in another subnet to represent logical interdependence.

(2) Points of interaction or commonality between the project activities and outside influences.

interface management

(1) Process of identifying, documenting, scheduling, communicating, and monitoring interfaces related to the product and the project. The three major types of interfaces are (1) personal and interpersonal, (2) organizational, and (3) system or technical.

(2) Management of communication, coordination, and responsibility between two organizations, phases, or physical entities that are interdependent.

interfaces

Boundary areas, often ill defined, between departments or functions.

internal audit

Self-audit conducted by members of the project team or a unit in the organization.

internal control

Process of monitoring and dealing with deviations from the project plan.

internal documentation

Written information that is associated with the development process, the quality system, and the product; is retained in the project files; and is not part of the final product.

internal project sources

Historical data on similar procurements, cost and performance data on various contractors, and other internal information used in a proposed procurement.

internal rate of return (IRR)

Annual rate of earnings on an investment. IRR equates the value of the cash returns with invested cash and considers the application of compound interest factors. The formula is as follows:

$$\sum^{n} \frac{\text{Periodic cash flow}}{(1+i)^t} = \text{Investment amount}$$

where i = internal rate of return, t = each time interval, n = total number of time intervals, and $\sum$ is summation.

internal risk
Risk under the control or influence of the project team. *See also* external risk.

International Project Management Association (IPMA)
Association of project management associations headquartered in Zurich, Switzerland, comprising, for the most part, European country project management associations. Has developed a four-level certification program for project managers.

International Standards Organization (ISO)
Voluntary organization consisting of national standardization bodies of each member country. Prepares and issues standards identified as "ISO-XXXX."

Internet portal
See portal.

Internet speed
Term used to describe the accelerating pace of modern business including, but not limited to, decision making, software development, project completion, and time-to-market.

interpersonal interfaces
Formal and informal reporting relationships among various project stakeholders.

intervenor
Alternative name for a stakeholder in the nuclear-power-plant-construction industry.

intimidating management style

Management approach in which the project manager frequently reprimands team members, to uphold his or her image as a demanding manager, at the risk of lowering team morale.

inventory closeout

Settlement and credit of inventory if purchased from project funds.

invitation for bid (IFB)

In U.S. federal government procurement, solicitation document used in sealed bidding procurements; generally, equivalent to a request for proposals.

invoice

(1) Written account or itemized statement addressed to the purchaser of merchandise shipped or services performed with the quantity, prices, and charges listed.
(2) Contractor's bill or written request for payment for work or services performed under the contract.

IPMA

See International Project Management Association.

IRR

See internal rate of return.

Ishikawa diagram

Diagram used to illustrate how various causes and subcauses create a specific effect. Named after its developer Kaoru Ishikawa. *Also called* cause-and-effect diagram *or* fishbone diagram.

ISO

See International Standards Organization.

ISO 9000

Set of documented standards to help organizations ensure that their quality systems meet certain minimal levels of consistent performance.

isomorphic team structure

Organization of a project team so that it closely reflects the physical structure of the project deliverable; for example, if the project is to produce a book, then each team member writes one chapter. The project manager is responsible for integrating the team's pieces into a cohesive final product.

issue

Formally identified item related to a project that, if not addressed, may—

- Affect its schedule
- Change its direction
- Diminish its quality
- Increase its cost

Distinguished from a risk in that it is an extant problem, whereas a risk is a future event. In many organizations, the terms are used interchangeably.

issue management

Structured, documented, and formal process or set of procedures used by an organization or a project to identify, categorize, and resolve issues. *See* issue.

IV&V

See independent verification and validation.

J

job description

Written outline, by job type, of the skills, responsibilities, knowledge, authority, and relationships involved in an individual's job. *Also called* position description.

job order

In U.S. federal government procurement, an order issued by a procuring authority for work to be done under the terms of a basic agreement, basic ordering agreement, or master agreement. Usually is a firm-fixed-price contract for a specific item of work.

joint venture

Contractual partnership between organizations for a particular transaction to achieve common goals for mutual profit. Differs from a partnership in that a joint venture does not entail a continuing relationship between the parties.

judicial management style

Management approach in which the project manager exercises sound judgment and applies it to project issues as the need arises.

just in time

Approach used to manage resources, requirements, and production so that the right material arrives at the right place at the right time, just in time for use.

K

Kaizen

Japanese term for continuous improvement.

Kanban technique

Method used to improve process flow by use of tags, status display boards, small designated material transfer spaces, designated containers, and similar mechanisms to give more visibility and control to the flow of material. Dedicated space is set up to limit the quantity of material that may be held to the amount calculated as appropriate for just-in-time processing. The limited number of dedicated containers also serves as a control or regulator on the rate of production, helping to reinforce the just-in-time demand-based system for material flow.

key event

See milestone.

key-event schedule

See milestone schedule.

kickoff meeting

Meeting held to acquaint stakeholders with the project and each other; presumes the presence of the customer and serves as an initial review of project scope and activities. Usually conducted after contract award or a decision to initiate a project.

kill point

See control gate.

kinesics

Study of communication through body movement.

KISS model

Pragmatic philosophy of conducting business in which the objective is to keep things, such as procedures, reports, and any other aspect of work, as simple as possible to get the job done. The acronym humorously describes the basic premise of simplicity, which is "keep it simple stupid."

Kiviat graph

Multifaceted graphic representation technique for displaying the results of many changing variables simultaneously. Used to display productivity, quality, and other targets together.

knowledge management

Collection of systems, processes, and procedures designed to acquire and share the intellectual assets of an organization. According to its proponents, knowledge management is the key that will give the organization a competitive advantage in the marketplace and enable it to serve its customers more efficiently. In project management, having a formal lessons-learned process is a form of knowledge management that can significantly aid project managers in avoiding the same mistakes others have made in the past.

knowledge transfer

Flow of knowledge, skills, information, and competencies from one person to another. Can happen through any number of methods including coaching, mentoring, training courses, and on-the-job experience.

L

labor
Effort expended by people for wages or salary. Generally classified as either direct or indirect. Direct labor is applied to meeting project objectives and is a principal element used in costing, pricing, and profit determination; indirect labor is a component of indirect cost, such as overhead or general and administrative costs.

labor efficiency
Ratio of earned hours to actual hours spent on a prescribed task during a reporting period. When earned hours equal actual hours, the efficiency equals 100 percent.

labor-hour contract
Type of contract in which a fixed amount is paid for each hour of work performed by a specific labor class.

lag
Modification of a logical relationship in a schedule such that there is a delay in the successor task. For example, in a finish-to-start dependency with a 5-day lag, the successor activity cannot start until 5 days after the predecessor has finished. *See also* lead.

lag relationship
One of four types of relationships involving a lag between the start or finish of a work item and the start or finish of another work item: (1) finish-to-start, (2) start-to-finish, (3) finish-to-finish, and (4) start-to-start.

laissez-faire management style
Management approach in which team members are not directed by management. Little information flows from the project team to the project manager, or vice versa. This style is

appropriate if the team is highly skilled and knowledgeable and wants no interference by the project manager.

late finish date (LF)

Latest possible point in time that an activity may end without a delay in the project finish date. Used in the critical path method. *See also* late start date.

late start date (LS)

Latest possible point in time that an activity may begin without delaying the project finish date. Used in the critical path method. *See also* late finish date.

lateral communication

Communication across lines of an organization of equivalent authority.

latest revised estimate

See estimate at completion.

law of diminishing returns

Economic theory stating that beyond a certain production or quality level, productivity or quality increases at a decreasing rate. Therefore, for every dollar invested in efforts to increase productivity, or quality, one can expect less than a dollar of productivity or quality gains in return.

lead

Modification of a logical relationship in a schedule such that there is an acceleration of the successor task. For example, in a finish-to-start dependency with a 5-day lead, the successor activity can start 5 days before the predecessor has finished. *See also* lag.

lead time

The time required to wait for a product, service, material, or resources, after ordering or making a request for such things.

leader

Individual who uses his or her influence in a group to motivate others to do something. Often used to refer to the project manager who is the individual vested with formal authority for achieving project aims.

leader-company contracting

U.S. federal government acquisition approach used to establish a second source for a product that is being or has been developed by a single contractor. *Also called* leader-follower procurement.

leader-follower procurement

See leader-company contracting.

leadership

(1) Use of influence to direct the activities of others toward the accomplishment of some objective.
(2) Ability to persuade others to do things enthusiastically.
(3) Human factor that binds a group together and motivates it toward goals.

leading

Establishing direction and aligning, motivating, and inspiring people.

learning curve

(1) Graphical or numerical relationship between the average cost or unit cost of an item and the quantity produced.
(2) Tool used to project the amount of direct labor or material that will be used to manufacture a product on a repetitive basis.

learning curve theory

Parametric model that says that each time we double the number of times we have performed a task, the time it takes to perform the task will decrease in a regular pattern.

learning rate

Percentage of worker hours per unit required to increase the output to a specified level.

legal opinion

Written statement by a lawyer describing what is legal or lawful in accordance with the governing laws of the land.

legitimate authority

See formal authority.

lessons learned

Documented information, usually collected through meetings, discussions, or written reports, to show how both common and uncommon project events were addressed. This information can be used by other project managers as a reference for subsequent project efforts.

lessons-learned review

Audit or evaluation conducted immediately upon project completion by the project team to learn from the successes and failures recently experienced. The results of the review are documented for use by project team members and other interested parties as a reference and guide for future project activities. *Also called* postproject evaluation and review.

letter contract

Preliminary, written contractual instrument that authorizes the immediate start of an activity under its terms and conditions before a pricing arrangement for the work to be done has been defined; a means to permit contractors to start work immediately after a requirement is identified.

level finish schedule

Date an activity is scheduled to end using the resource allocation process.

level of approval

Management level at which approvals are given.

level of effort (LOE)

Support-type activity (such as vendor or customer liaison) that does not readily lend itself to measurement of discrete accomplishment and is generally characterized by a uniform rate of activity over a specific time period.

level start schedule

Date activity is scheduled to begin using the resource allocation process. Equal to or later in time than the early start.

leveling

See resource leveling.

level-of-effort contract

Type of contract stating the amount of work in terms of effort, usually person-hours, person-months, or person-years, to be performed by specified labor classes over a given period of time.

level-of-effort cost account

Cost account that is necessary to a project but is more time oriented than task oriented. Examples include project management, scheduling, and field engineering support. When these functions are charged directly to a contract, they continue for the life of the project but have no measurable output.

LF

See late finish date.

liability period

Time during which a prime contractor or subcontractor is liable for a failure of a product that has been delivered.

license

Official grant of permission needed to do a particular thing, exercise a certain privilege, or engage in a particular business or occupation. Licenses may be granted by governments, businesses, or individuals.

licensing agreement

Arrangement whereby an organization that owns specific technology or information authorizes its use by another organization under certain conditions.

life cycle

The entire useful life of a product or service, usually divided into sequential phases, which include initiation, development, execution, operation, maintenance, and disposal or termination. *See also* project life cycle.

life-cycle cost
The sum total of all costs associated with the life cycle, including developing, acquiring, operating, supporting, and (if applicable) disposing of the product or service developed or acquired so decisions can be made among alternatives. *See also* project life-cycle cost.

limitation of funds
Sum of funds available for expenses beyond which no work can be authorized for performance during a specified period.

limitation-of-cost clause
Key clause in cost-reimbursement contracts to obligate the contractor to use its best efforts to perform the specified work and all obligations under the contract within the target, or estimated, cost.

limitation-of-funds clause
Clause included in all incrementally funded cost-reimbursement contracts specifying that a contractor must notify the buyer in writing when the contractor determines that additional funds must be allotted to the contract to continue or to complete performance.

limiting quality
Maximum number of defects in product quality (or the worst product quality) that the consumer is willing to accept at a specified probability of occurrence.

line function
That part of a corporation that is responsible for producing its goods or performing its services. *See also* line manager.

line item
(1) Smallest unit of a product whose status is tracked in a status system and which is usually a deliverable.
(2) Item of supply or service for which the contractor must bid a separate price.

line manager

Manager of a group that makes a product or performs a service. *Also called* functional manager.

line of balance

Technique used to interpret and present graphically the essential factors involved in a production process from selection and assembly of raw materials to completion of the end product against time. The flow of materials and components is integrated into manufacture of end items according to phased delivery requirements. The technique provides information on project status, showing progress, timing, and phasing of related project activities, but lacks predictive features. It is most useful in production programs from the point when incoming or raw materials are received to the time end products are shipped.

line organization

See line function.

linear organization chart

Used in addition to an organization chart to show the work package position in the organization by showing who participates, and to what extent, when an activity is performed or a decision is made. Shows the extent or type of authority exercised by each person in performing an activity in which two or more people have overlapping involvement.

link

See logical relationship.

linked activity

Activity dependent on the performance of another activity in precedence diagramming.

liquidated damages

Express provision in a contract that specifies a sum for which one of the parties will be liable upon breach of contract or failure to perform.

loaded rates
Charges for human and material resources that incorporate both hourly or per-use charges and all additional general and administrative costs associated with their use.

loading factor
Scheduling allowance to adjust for project rework, administrative, nonproject, and nature-of-the-work time.

LOE
See level of effort.

logic
See network logic.

logic diagram
See network diagram.

logical relationship
Dependency between two project activities or between a project activity and a milestone. The four types of logical relationships in the precedence diagramming method are (1) finish-to-start—the "from" activity must finish before the "to" activity can start, (2) finish-to-finish—the "from" activity must finish before the "to" activity can finish, (3) start-to-start—the "from" activity must start before the "to" activity can start, and (4) start-to-finish—the "from" activity must start before the "to" activity can finish. *Also called* link.

loop
Network path that passes the same node twice. Loops cannot be analyzed using network analysis techniques such as CPM and PERT but are allowed in GERT.

lose-lose
Outcome of conflict resolution that results in both parties being worse off than before. Based on the strategy that it is better for each party to get something than nothing, even if that something does not accomplish either party's goals.

loss

Failure to earn a profit on a contract because the costs of performance (both direct and indirect) have exceeded the amount paid to the contractor under the terms of the contract.

lot

Collection of units of product identified and treated as a unique entity from which a sample can be drawn and inspected to determine whether there is conformance with acceptability criteria. *Also called* batch.

lot formation

Process of collecting, segregating, or delineating production units into homogeneous, identifiable groups by type, grade, class, size, composition, or condition of manufacture.

lot size

Number of units of product that constitute a lot.

low balling

See buying in.

low-ball offer

Artificially low-priced bid offered by a seller to induce a buyer to select him or her, over other competitors, to perform the service or provide the products required. Once the bid is won, the seller attempts to earn what is actually required to do the job by negotiating artificially high-priced change orders during the contract or work period.

lowest overall cost

Considering price and other factors, the least expenditure of funds over the life cycle of a system or an item.

lowest responsive, responsible bidder

In U.S. federal government procurement, a contractor in a sealed bid procurement that is entitled to receive the contract award.

LS

See late start date.

M

maintainability

Design and installation characteristic expressed as the probability that a specified condition will be restored in a given period of time when maintenance is performed according to prescribed procedures and resources.

maintenance guarantee

Assurance that a product will be maintained during a specified period of time.

maintenance quality assurance

Determination that material maintained, overhauled, rebuilt, modified, or reclaimed conforms to the prescribed technical requirements.

major defect

Defect that is not critical but is still likely to result in failure or will materially reduce the usability of the unit of product for its intended purpose.

major defective

Product unit that contains one or more major defects and may also contain minor defects but does not contain a critical defect.

make-or-buy analysis

Management technique used to determine whether a particular product or service can be produced or performed cost-effectively by the performing organization or should be contracted out to another organization. The analysis considers both the direct costs of procuring the product or service and any administrative costs in managing the contractor.

Malcolm Baldrige National Quality Award

Established by the U.S. Department of Commerce and administered by the National Institute of Standards and Technology, this award is presented annually to U.S. corporations in various categories that have demonstrated a commitment to quality. Nominees complete a detailed application that solicits specific information regarding their quality activities in the following categories: leadership; strategic planning; customer and market focus; information and analysis; human resource focus; process management; and business results.

management by exception
Management approach in which managers concern themselves with only those variances that appear exceptionally large, significant, or otherwise peculiar.

management by objectives (MBO)
Management approach or methodology, developed by Peter Drucker in the early 1950s, that encourages managers to give their subordinates more freedom in determining how to achieve specific objectives. Management and the subordinate jointly develop clear objectives, requirements, and milestones and ensure that they are realistic, measurable, and achievable. Subordinate performance and compensation are measured by progress achieved against these goals at regular intervals.

management by projects
Management approach that treats many aspects of ongoing operations in an organization as projects, applying project management principles and practices to them.

management plan
Document that describes the overall guidelines under which the project is organized, administered, and managed to ensure timely accomplishment of project objectives.

management reserve
Separately planned quantity of money or time intended to reduce the impact of missed cost, schedule, or performance objectives, which are impossible to plan for (sometimes called "unknown unknowns").

management style
One of the following management approaches that a project manager may adopt depending on the situation: authoritarian,

autocratic, combative, conciliatory, consensual, consultative-autocratic, democratic, disruptive, ethical, facilitating, intimidating, judicial, laissez-faire, participative, promotional, secretive, shared leadership, or shareholder manager style. *See individual entries for definitions of each management style.*

managerial quality administration
Process of defining and monitoring policies, responsibilities, and systems that are necessary to ensure that quality standards are met throughout the project.

mandatory dependency
Dependency inherent in the nature of the work being done, such as a physical limitation. *Also called* hard logic.

margin
Gain accrued over and above the cost of the product or service delivered.

marginal cost
Increase or decrease in cost based on the result of one more or one less unit of output. Used to determine the value of increasing or decreasing production, or assigning additional personnel to a project.

market requirements
List of needs that describes the business environment in which a product or service is targeted to be sold.

market survey
Collection and analysis of data from potential sellers to determine the capability of satisfying buyer requirements. Includes activities such as writing or calling knowledgeable experts, reviewing catalogs and marketing brochures, attending demonstrations, or conducting a formal request for information.

Markov chain
Method used to evaluate a system's mean time until failure. The system is modeled as a finite-state machine with working

states and fault states, and a probability is associated with the transitions between states.

Maslow's hierarchy of needs

Theory of motivation developed by Abraham Maslow in which a person's needs arise in an ordered sequence in the following five categories: (1) physical needs, (2) safety needs, (3) love needs, (4) esteem needs, and (5) self-actualization needs.

master schedule

See milestone schedule.

material breach

Discharge of the nonfaulted party from any further obligations under the contract. The most serious form of breach. *See also* breach.

material requirements planning (MRP)

Planning and material-ordering technique based on the known or forecast final-demand requirements for each item, lead times for each fabricated or purchased item, and existing inventories of all items.

material review board

Formal board established in many U.S. federal government procurements to review, evaluate, and dispose of specific nonconforming supplies or services and to ensure that corrective action is initiated and accomplished so future nonconformances do not occur.

materials management

Organizational process, procedures, rules, and regulations for the ordering, storage, and movement of materials.

mathematical programming

Category of mathematical techniques for solving resource allocation and other constrained optimization problems; includes, for example, integer and linear programming.

matrix organization

Project organizational structure in which the project manager shares responsibility with the functional managers to assign priorities and direct the work of individuals assigned to the project. In a strong matrix organization, the balance of power over the resources is in favor of the project manager. In a weak matrix organization, functional managers retain most of the control over project resources.

maturity level

A defined position in an achievement scale that establishes the attainment of certain capabilities.

maximum fee

Dollar amount negotiated in a cost-plus-incentive fee contract as the maximum amount of profit that the contractor can receive.

MBO

See management by objectives.

McGregor's Theory X and Y

Theory of motivation advanced by Douglas McGregor, which holds that managers have a tendency to hold two bipolar sets of assumptions about workers. Theory X managers view workers as machines who require a great deal of external control. Theory Y managers view workers as organisms who grow, develop, and exercise control over themselves.

m-commerce (mobile commerce)

Conducting business-to-consumer transactions, usually over the Internet, using wireless, mobile devices such as cellular telephones, electronic organizers, personal digital assistants, and other forms of electronic apparatus. Such wireless Internet access requires the use of wireless application protocol (WAP), the standard used for such electronic communications.
Examples of m-commerce applications include receiving stock quotes, driving directions, or locations of the nearest coffee bar through a cellular telephone.

mean down time

Measure of maintainability derived by dividing the sum of the elapsed clock time that a system or product is unavailable due to failures by the number of occurrences over a selected time frame, usually 1 year.

mean time between failure (MTBF)

Measure of maintainability derived by dividing the sum of elapsed clock time between system failures by the number of occurrences over a selected time frame, usually 1 year.

mean time to repair (MTTR)

Measure of maintainability derived by dividing the sum of the elapsed clock time to perform corrective actions by the number of corrective actions required in a selected time frame, usually 1 year.

measurement of cost

Accounting methods and techniques used to define cost components, determine the basis for cost measurement, and establish criteria for use of alternative cost measurement techniques.

measuring and test equipment

Devices used to measure, gauge, test, inspect, diagnose, or otherwise examine materials, supplies, and equipment to determine whether they comply with technical requirements.

mediation

Process of bringing parties engaged in a dispute or disagreement together to settle their differences through a meeting with a disinterested party, the mediator. Unlike binding arbitration, the mediator has no authority to force a settlement.

meeting of the minds

Mutual assent of the parties to a contract, agreement, or course of action.

mega-project
Extremely large and complex project (US$100 million+) designed to accomplish an extensive scope of activities and requiring many more resources than most projects.

merchantability
Fitness for a particular purpose. Used to measure implied warranties. Products are merchantable if they are reasonably fit for ordinary purposes for which the goods are to be used.

methodology
See project management methodology.

metrics
Units of measurement used to assess, calculate, or determine, progress performance in terms of monetary units, schedule, or quality results.

microculture
Specific culture that exists within a particular organizational unit or the project.

midpoint pricing
Using a single set of rates that are the weighted average of a future time period rather than using progressively escalated rates to develop an escalated price estimate.

migration
Movement of files and data between software applications.

migration planning
Developing a plan to move from one software environment to another.

milestone
(1) Event with a zero duration and requiring no resources. Used to measure the progress of a project and signifies completion or start of a major deliverable or other significant metric such as costs incurred, hours used, payment made, and so on.

(2) Identifiable point in a project or set of activities that represents a reporting requirement or completion of a large or important set of activities. *Also called* key event.

milestone chart
Scheduling technique used to show the start and completion of milestones on a time-scale chart. Normally, planned events are expressed using hollow triangles, and completed events are shown as solid triangles. Rescheduled or slipped events are usually displayed as hollow diamond symbols. When the late milestones are completed, the diamonds are filled in. *Also called* event chart.

milestone method
Approach to calculating earned value, which works well when work packages exceed 3 months in duration. First, objective milestones are established, preferably one or more for each month of the project. Then, the assigned work package budget is divided, based on a weighted value assigned to each milestone.

milestone schedule
Schedule consisting of key events or milestones (generally, critical accomplishments planned at time intervals throughout the project) and used to monitor overall project performance. May be either a network or bar chart and usually contains minimal detail at a highly summarized level. *Also called* key event schedule, master schedule *or* summary schedule.

milestones for control
Establishing interim schedule objectives to measure progress.

minimum fee
Dollar amount negotiated in a cost-plus-incentive fee contract as the minimum amount of profit that the contractor can receive.

minor defect
(1) Defect that probably will not materially reduce the usability of the unit of product or the project for its intended purpose.

(2) Departure from established standards that has minimal impact on the effective use or operation of the unit.

minor defective
Unit of product that contains one or more minor defects, but none of these defects are critical or major.

minor risk
Risk event that does not cause significant problems, no matter what its probability.

mission
Specific purpose that all or part of the organization is dedicated to achieving.

mission statement
Description prepared and endorsed by members of the organization that answers these questions: What do we do? For whom do we do it? How do we go about it? Used as a guide for making decisions in projects.

mitigation
Risk response strategy that decreases risk by lowering the probability of a risk event's occurrence or reducing the effect of the risk should it occur. *See also* acceptance *and* avoidance.

mitigation strategy
Carefully organized steps taken to reduce or eliminate the probability of a risk's occurring or the impact of a risk on a project.

mixed organization
Organizational structure that includes both functions (disciplines) and projects in its hierarchy.

mock-up
Physical or virtual demonstration model, built to scale, and used early in the development of a project to verify proposed design, fit, critical clearances, operator interfaces, and other physical characteristics of the item to be produced.

model

Way to look at an item, generally by abstracting and simplifying it to make it understandable in a particular context.

modern project management (MPM)

Broad range of project management activities (scope, cost, time, quality, risk, and so on) as distinguished from the narrower, traditional view of project management that focuses only on cost and time.

modification

Change to a project's scope or the terms of a contract; usually written. Examples are change orders, notices of termination, supplemental agreements, and exercises of contract options.

moments of truth (MOT)

Point in time when a customer comes into contact with the products, systems, people, or procedures of an organization, resulting in a judgment of the quality of the organization's product or service. First articulated by Jan Carlzon when head of Scandinavian Airlines.

monitor

Acquire and analyze data on an ongoing basis so that action can be taken when progress fails to match plans and meet objectives.

monitoring actuals versus budget

Continually measuring actual cost against the budget to establish the variance, analyze the reasons for the variance, and take the necessary corrective action. Also, monitoring, managing, and controlling changes in the final cost.

Monte Carlo analysis

Schedule or cost risk assessment technique that entails performing a project simulation many times to calculate a likely distribution of results. *See also* schedule simulation.

most likely time

In PERT estimating, the most realistic number of work periods the activity will consume.

MOT
See moments of truth.

motivating
Inducing an individual to work toward his or her goals.

Motivation-Hygiene Theory
Theory of motivation described by Frederick Herzberg, which asserts that two sets of factors must be considered to satisfy a person's needs: (1) those related to job satisfaction (motivators) and (2) those related to job dissatisfaction (hygiene or maintenance factors). To retain employees, managers must focus on improving negative hygiene factors (such as pay), but to get employees to devote a higher level of energy to their work, managers must use motivators (such as recognition).

motivators
According to Frederick Herzberg's Motivation-Hygiene Theory, factors related to job satisfaction that must be addressed to motivate employees, such as recognition or greater responsibility. *See also* Motivation-Hygiene Theory.

moving average cost
Inventory costing method in which an average unit cost is computed after each acquisition by adding the cost of newly acquired units to the cost of the units of inventory on hand and dividing this number by the new total number of units.

MPM
See modern project management.

MRP
See material requirements planning.

multidisciplinary
Encompassing effort by many types of people representing different skills and backgrounds in the organization.

multiple-project scheduling
Process of developing a project schedule based on constraints imposed by other projects.

multiyear contracting

Special contracting method covering more than 1 year of requirements, but the total funds to be obligated are not available at the time of contract award.

Murphy's law

Informal and unfounded principle of business stating that whatever can go wrong will go wrong. Ed Murphy, a development engineer, coined the term in 1949 as a result of errors made by a laboratory technician.

Myers-Briggs Type Indicator

Test developed by Katharine C. Briggs and Isabel Briggs Myers to categorize people according to where they lie on four scales, each reflecting a different dimension of human behavior: extrovert-introvert, sensing-intuitive, thinking-feeling, and judging-perceiving. These scales comprise 16 different psychological types, each associated with a number of well-documented behavioral traits.

N

natural variation

Quality concept that asserts that making any product or delivering any service with absolute consistency is impossible. This type of variation can be predicted through the application of statistical techniques.

near-critical activity

Activity that has little total float or that otherwise could become critical as a result of certain situations occurring.

near-term activity

Activity that will either begin, be in process, or be completed during a relatively short period of time.

needs requirements life cycle

Process of identifying and articulating needs of the intended users, sponsors, or beneficiaries of a project to ensure that the project will satisfy those needs. Comprising several steps, this

cycle begins when needs first emerge and ends when those
needs are subsequently articulated either in functional or
technical terms.

negative cash flow

Situation in which a business is spending more than it is
earning in any given accounting period.

negative float

Situation in which the difference between the late (start or
finish) date and early (start or finish) date of an activity is a
negative number, indicating that the late date is earlier in time
than the early date. This situation comes into existence when a
forced end date of an activity is used to calculate the backward
pass without considering the predecessor activity's start date
and duration. Negative float means the activity cannot be
completed on time unless and until certain decisions are made
to correct the situation.

negotiated bidding rates

Rates agreed to with the customer based on a reasonable
projection of the direct costs as related to a projection of the
indirect costs, usually reaching 3 years into the future. *See also*
forward pricing.

negotiated final rates

Actual rates agreed-upon by the customer after the fact. Actual
costs are adjusted to exclude those items that the customer
refuses to allow, such as entertainment costs.

negotiating

(1) Process of bargaining with individuals concerning
resources, information, and activities. Conferring with others
to come to terms or reach an agreement.
(2) Process in which parties with different interests reach an
acceptable agreement through communication and
compromise.

net book value

Dollar amount shown in the accounting system for assets, liabilities, or equity. When comparing one company to another, net book value is the excess of total assets over total liabilities.

net loss

Situation in which the expenses for an accounting period exceed income.

net present value (NPV)

Financial calculation that takes into account the time values of a stream of income and expenditure at a given interest rate.

net profit

Amount of money earned after all expenses, including direct and indirect costs, have been deducted from total revenue.

network

(1) Graphic depiction of the relationships of project work (activities or tasks). *See also* network diagram.
(2) Communication facility that connects end systems; interconnected series of points, nodes, or stations connected by communication channels; or assembly of equipment through which connections are made between data stations.

network analysis

Identification of early and late start and finish dates for uncompleted portions of project activities. *Also called* schedule analysis. *See also* critical path method, Program Evaluation and Review Technique, *and* Graphical Evaluation and Review Technique.

network diagram

Schematic display of the logical relationships of project activities, usually drawn from left to right to reflect project chronology. *Also called* logic diagram *and* often incorrectly referred to as a PERT chart.

network logic
Sequence of activities in a network affecting the order in which the work will be performed.

network path
Continuous series of connected activities in a project network diagram.

network-based scheduling
Process of determining logical relationships among WBS work packages, activities, and tasks and then arranging same to establish the shortest possible project duration. Examples of these techniques include PERT, CPM, and PDM.

node
Junction point joined to some or all of the other dependency lines in a network; an intersection of two or more lines or arrows. *See also* arrow diagramming method *and* precedence diagramming method.

nominal group technique
Specific structured process of team brainstorming and creative problem solving that draws on individual and group strengths but prevents domination by any one individual. Consists of five separate steps as follows: (1) silent generation—individual team members write responses to a problem statement in silence; (2) round robin—each team member recites his or her responses, which are written on a chart; (3) clarification—the group discusses the remarks; (4) selection and ranking—each team member selects and ranks in priority order the top 3 to 10 ideas collected; and (5) final selection and ranking—the facilitator tallies the results and prepares the group's ranked set of ideas.

nominal rate
Rate of return on an investment that is unadjusted for inflation.

nonbinding arbitration
Arbitration in which the parties are not legally bound to the decision of the arbitrator. *See also* arbitration.

nonconformance
Deficiency in characteristics, documentation, or procedures that makes the quality of material, service, or product unacceptable or indeterminate.

nondisclosure agreement
Legally binding document in which an organization promises to use another's proprietary data only for specific purposes and not to reveal or disclose these data to any other organization or individual.

nonpersonal services contract
Contract under which the personnel performing the services are not subject, either by the contract's terms or by the manner of its administration, to the supervision and control that usually exist between the buyer and its employees.

nonrecurring cost
Project-incurred cost that is not expected to recur on any future work.

nonwork unit
Calendar unit in which certain types of work will not be performed on an activity, such as holidays.

normal inspection
Inspection, under a sampling plan, that is used when no evidence exists that the quality level of the product being submitted is better or worse than the specified quality level.

normative forecasting
Method for assessing the future in terms of what is required to reach a particular objective. Used in gap analysis for determining the contents of a project portfolio to ensure that the objective can be achieved.

not invented here syndrome (NIH)
Attitude that prevents individuals and groups from using and benefiting from the ideas of other individuals or groups because of personal pride; cultural, ethnic, or national prejudice; or other bias.

NPV
See net present value.

O

objective
(1) End toward which effort is directed; a predetermined result.
(2) Organizational performance criteria to be achieved and measured in the use of organizational resources.

objective quality evidence
Statement of fact, either quantitative or qualitative, about the quality of a product or service based on observations, measurements, or tests that can be verified. Evidence describing the item, process, or procedure can be expressed in terms of specific quality requirements or characteristics that are identified in drawings, specifications, and other documents.

OBS
See organizational breakdown structure.

offer
Response to a solicitation that, if accepted, would bind the contractor to perform the resulting contract.

offeror
Party who makes an offer and looks for acceptance from the buyer.

off-the-shelf item
Item produced and placed in stock by a manufacturer or contractor or stocked by a distributor before orders or contracts are received for its sale.

one hundred percent inspection
Inspection where specific characteristics of each product unit are examined or tested to determine conformance with requirements.

one-stop, all-stop flow control

Production approach in which coordination and communication among process stages are regulated as a balanced flow process. All stages of a process function together as a unit. If one stage of the process has a major problem and must shut down for correction, all other stages of the process will automatically stop after reaching a predetermined quantity of completed work in the holding area.

open-door policy

Management approach that encourages employees to speak freely and regularly to management regarding any aspect of the business or project. Adopted to promote the open flow of communication and to increase the success of business operations or project performance by soliciting the ideas of employees. Tends to minimize personnel problems and employee dissatisfaction.

open-ended problem

Problem without a single correct answer, with boundaries that can be challenged.

operating characteristic curve

Plotted curve showing the percent of lots or batches that may be expected to be accepted under a specific sampling plan for a given process quality.

operation phase

See implementation phase.

operational definition

Description in specific terms of what something is and how it is measured by the quality control process. May include metrics.

operations and maintenance (O&M)

Phase in the product life cycle that immediately follows the acceptance of the product by the end-user, sponsor, or client. Responsibility for this phase typically rests with the product manager, not the project manager.

opportunity
(1) Future event or series of events that, if occurring, will have a positive impact on the project.
(2) Benefit to be realized from undertaking a project.

opportunity assessment
Examination of the uncertainty associated with the possible occurrence of an event that is expected to have a positive impact on a project.

opportunity cost
Rate of return that would have been earned by selecting an alternative project rather than the one selected. Opportunity cost is used as one variable in project selection.

optimistic time
In PERT estimating, the minimum number of work periods the activity will consume.

optimization strategy
Carefully organized steps used to maximize the occurrence or impact of a project opportunity.

order-of-magnitude estimate
Approximate estimate that is accurate to within –25 to +75 percent and is made without detailed data. Usually produced from a cost capacity curve, with scale-up or scale-down factors that are appropriately escalated, and approximate cost capacity ratios. Used in the formative stages of an expenditure program for initial project evaluation. *Also called* preliminary, conceptual, *or* feasibility estimate. *See also* estimate.

organization
Company, corporation, firm, or enterprise, either public or private, which may or may not be incorporated.

organization chart
Graphic display of reporting relationships that provide a general framework of the organization.

organization cost
Cost relating to business organization or reorganization expenses, such as incorporation fees and costs of attorneys, accountants, brokers, promoters, organizers, management consultants, and investment counselors, whether or not they are employees of the organization.

organizational breakdown structure (OBS)
Tool used to show the work units or work packages that are assigned to specific organizational units.

organizational interfaces
Formal and informal reporting and working relationships among different organizational units.

organizational planning
Process of identifying, documenting, and assigning project roles, responsibilities, and reporting relationships.

organizational resources
Human and nonhuman resources available to the organization to fulfill its mission, objectives, and goals.

organizational strategy
Means through which the use of resources accomplishes end purposes.

organizational structure
Alignment of human resources and functions of the organization.

original duration
First estimate of the number of work units needed to complete an activity. Most common time units are hours, days, weeks, and months.

original inspection
First inspection of a particular quantity of product as distinguished from the inspection of a product that has been resubmitted after prior rejection.

other bid considerations

Evaluation of the organization's personnel and financial resources, facilities, performance record, responsiveness to contract terms and conditions, and general willingness to perform the work.

other direct costs

Group of accounting elements that can be attributed to specific tasks or activities. Examples include travel, living, and postage costs.

output

Documents or deliverable items that are a result of a process.

outsourcing

Process of awarding a contract or otherwise entering into an agreement with a third party, usually a supplier, to perform services that are currently being performed by an organization's employees. Organizations "outsource" elements of their operations for one or both of the following reasons: (1) The service can be performed cheaper, faster, or better by a third party. (2) The service (for example, janitorial services) is not a core business function contributing to the revenue growth and technical expertise of the organization. Accordingly, management does not want to focus time and attention on it. *See also* contracting out.

overall change control

(1) Activities concerned with influencing the factors that create changes to ensure that they are beneficial, determining that a change has occurred, and managing the actual changes when and as they occur. *See also* change control.

(2) Coordination of changes across the entire project.

overhead cost

See (2) under indirect cost.

overhead rate

Percentage rate determined by dividing an organization's indirect cost pool for an accounting period by the base used to allocate indirect costs to work accomplished during the period of performance.

overrun
Amount of the cost of performance that is greater than the amount estimated.

overtime
Time worked by an employee in excess of the agreed-upon normal working hours. Typically compensated for by either a higher rate of pay per hour or compensatory time.

ownership of quality responsibility
Ultimate responsibility of the individual performing a task to ensure that the requirements or specifications are met.

P

pairwise comparison
Multivoting technique used to rank-order a set of factors (for example, requirements, projects, and so on) when the members of a group cannot reach agreement on the priorities of each of the factors. Each factor is compared to every other factor and voted on by the group to determine which of the two compared is most important. After all the comparisons and voting are complete, the votes are tallied. The factor with the largest number of votes is the group's highest priority with the other factors ranked by descending order of votes.

parallel tasks
Independent tasks that proceed concurrently.

parametric cost estimating
Estimating approach that uses a statistical relationship between historical data and other variables (for example, lines of code in software development) to calculate an estimate.

parametric modeling
Project characteristics (parameters) used in a mathematical model to predict project costs. Considered to be reliable when

the historical information used to develop the model is accurate, parameters used in the model are readily quantifiable, and the model is scalable.

parent organization
Firm or organization within which the project is being conducted.

Pareto diagram
Histogram, ordered by frequency of occurrence, that shows the number of results that were generated by each identified cause. Usually includes a second scale to reflect percentage of results for each cause.

Pareto optimal solution
Solution in which making a party better off requires making another party worse off by the same or a greater amount.

Pareto's law
Principle, espoused by Joseph Juran and based on the work of nineteenth century Italian economist Vilfredo Pareto, stating that a relatively small number of causes typically will produce a large majority of problems or defects. Improvement efforts are usually most cost-effective when focused on a few high-impact causes.

partial audit
Audit that includes a subset of the project elements.

partial payment
Payment made upon delivery and acceptance of one or more complete deliverables or units as required under the contract even though other quantities or items remain to be delivered.

participative estimating
Estimating approach in which the primary estimator depends on other people to provide or review estimates for part or all of a work estimate.

participative management style
Management approach in which the project manager solicits information from and shares decision-making authority with the project team.

partnering
Approach used at the beginning of the contract that encourages assimilation of the contractor's employees into the project as full partners to achieve contract objectives.

partnership
Formal, legally structured working relationship of two or more parties to achieve common business goals.

party-at-interest
See project stakeholder.

patchwork deliverables
(1) Deliverables that lack cohesiveness, reflecting many ad hoc decisions rather than a comprehensive vision.
(2) Deliverables that are the result of a requirements definition method in which specifications are developed as they occur.

path
Set of sequentially connected tasks, activities, lines, or nodes in a project network diagram.

path convergence
Point at which parallel paths of a series of activities meet. Notable because of the tendency to delay the completion of the milestone where the paths meet.

path float
See float.

pay period
Specific period of time used to determine the pay earned by an employee. Pay periods are one week, two weeks, or monthly in most organizations.

payback period
Financial project evaluation criterion used to determine the amount of time before the net cash flow from a project becomes positive. *Also called* payout time period.

pay-for-performance
Compensation scheme for employees and team members in which their level of pay is directly tied to specific business goals and management objectives. Organizations adopt this approach to improve individual accountability; align shareholder, management, and employee interests; and enhance performance.

payment
Obligation to compensate the contractor according to the terms of the contract.

payment authorization
Process of allocated fund transfer to an account to pay the contractor for delivered goods or services according to contractual terms.

payment bond
Bond to secure the payment of subcontractors, laborers, and so on, by the prime contractor.

payout time period
See payback period.

PC
See percent complete.

PDCA
See plan-do-check-act cycle.

PDM
See precedence diagramming method.

PDR
See preliminary design review.

peer audit
Audit conducted by a group of peers rather than full-time or assigned auditors.

peer review
Review of a project or phase of a project by individuals with equivalent knowledge and background who are not currently members of the project team and have not participated in the development of the project.

percent complete (PC)
Estimate, expressed as a percent, of the amount of work completed on an activity or group of activities, typically based on resource use. Used in calculating earned value.

percent defective
Percent of defectives of any given quantity of units of product. Calculated by 100 times the number of defective units of product divided by the total number of units of product. *See also* defective.

performance
Determination of achievement, to measure and manage project quality.

performance bond
Bond used to secure the performance and fulfillment of all the undertakings, terms, and conditions of the contract.

performance improvement
Primary output of project team development, which may manifest itself in improvements in individual and team skills, behaviors, and capabilities.

performance measurement baseline
Time-phased budget plan used to measure performance. Formed by the budgets assigned to scheduled cost accounts and the applicable indirect budgets.

performance reporting

Collecting and disseminating information about project performance to provide project stakeholders with information about how resources are being used to achieve project objectives. Includes status reporting, progress reporting, and forecasting.

performance review

Meeting held periodically to assess project status or progress.

performance specification

Technical requirement that describes the operational characteristics desired for an item to convey what the final product should be capable of accomplishing rather than how it should be built or what its measurements, tolerances, or other design characteristics should be. If a contract contains performance specifications, the contractor accepts general responsibility for product design and engineering and for achieving the performance requirements in the contract.

performing organization

Enterprise whose employees are most involved in doing the project work.

personal services contract

Contract that by its express terms or as administered makes the contractor's personnel appear to be, in effect, employees of the buyer's organization.

PERT

See Program Evaluation and Review Technique.

PERT chart

Specific type of project network diagram. *See also* Program Evaluation and Review Technique.

PERT estimating

See Program Evaluation and Review Technique.

pessimistic duration

In PERT estimating, the maximum number of work periods the activity will consume. *Also called* pessimistic time.

pessimistic time

See pessimistic duration.

phase

See project phase.

phase exit

See control gate.

phased planning

Approach used to plan only to the level of detail that is known at the time. The output of each project phase includes a phase plan and an updated project plan. The phase plan is prepared at the task or work package level and provides the detailed work to be done in the next phase of the project; the updated project plan is the overall plan for the remainder of the project.

phase-end review

See control gate.

pilot

Trial apparatus or operation used to validate a proposed solution in a live environment.

plan

Intended future course of action.

plan-do-check-act (PDCA) cycle

Universal improvement methodology, advanced by W. Edwards Deming and based on the work of Walter Shewart, designed to continually improve the processes by which an organization produces a product or delivers a service.

planned activity

Activity or task that has not started or finished prior to the current date.

planned finish date
See scheduled finish date.

planned start date
See scheduled start date.

planning package
Logical aggregation of work within a cost account that can be identified and budgeted in early baseline planning but is not yet defined into work packages.

planning phase
See development phase.

planning processes
Activities associated with devising and maintaining a workable scheme to accomplish the business need that the project was undertaken to address.

platform
The hardware and systems software on which applications software is developed or installed and operated.

plug date
Date externally assigned to an activity that establishes the earliest or latest date the activity is allowed to start or finish.

PM
See project management.

PMBOK®
See project management body of knowledge.

PMI®
See Project Management Institute, Inc.

PMIS
See project management information system.

PMO
See program management office.

PMP®

See project management professional.

point of contact (POC)

Agreed to, official communication point between two interfacing organizations. Usually one person. *Also called* single point of contact.

policy deployment

Process of developing and promulgating policies in the organization; translating senior management's objectives into more specific and quantifiable objectives for each unit in the organization.

portal

Web site designed to provide a broad array of services, information, and references on a specific topic through a combination of its own content as well as links to other Web sites. As a "doorway" to the Web, a portal typically, but not always, provides these services for free with the expectation that visitors to the site will buy products and services from the organizations who advertise on the site.

position description

See job description.

positional negotiation

Negotiating approach in which immediate needs are stated on the assumption that the environment will not, or cannot, change.

postcontract evaluation

Objective review and analysis of both parties' performance, the technical problems encountered, and the corrective actions taken.

postproject analysis and report

Formal analysis and documentation of the project's results including cost, schedule, and technical performance versus the original plan.

postproject evaluation and review
See lessons learned review.

preaward meetings
Meetings to rank prospective contractors before final contract award and examine the contractors' facilities or capabilities.

preaward survey
Evaluation of a prospective contractor's capability to perform under the terms of a proposed contract.

prebid conference
See bidders conference.

precedence diagramming method (PDM)
Network diagramming technique in which activities are represented by boxes (or nodes) and linked by precedence relationship lines to show the sequence in which the activities are to be performed. The nodes are connected with arrows to show the dependencies. Four types of relationships are possible: finish-to-finish, finish-to-start, start-to-finish, and start-to-start. *Also called* activity-on-node (AON) *or* activity-on-arc.

precedence relationship
Term used in PDM for a logical relationship.

precontract cost
Cost incurred by a contractor before the contract's effective date.

predecessor activity
Activity or task that must begin or end before another activity or task can begin or end. (1) In ADM, the activity that enters a node. (2) In PDM, the "from" activity.

prefeasibility phase
See concept phase.

preferential logic
See discretionary dependency.

preferred logic

See discretionary dependency.

preliminary danger analysis

Technique in which the potential danger of each system component is identified. No cause-effect link is drawn between components and dangers. Generally used as the basis for other dependability techniques.

preliminary design review (PDR)

Review, conducted during system acquisition, of each configuration item to (1) evaluate the selected design approach in terms of progress, technical adequacy, and risk resolution; (2) determine the item's compatibility with the development specification's performance and engineering requirements; and (3) establish the existence and compatibility of the physical and functional interfaces among the item and other items in the project.

preliminary estimate

See order-of-magnitude estimate.

premature termination

Situation in which a decision is made to terminate a project before its objectives have been met. Many reasons exist for it, but generally speaking, it is an action taken by management because either the project cannot be completed within a reasonable time and cost range, or the end product or service of the project is no longer needed.

preproposal conference

In U.S. federal government procurement, a meeting held by the contracting officer with prospective contractors during the solicitation period of a procurement by negotiation.

prequalification

Determination of the contractor's responsibility prior to solicitation.

present value
Value in current monetary units of work to be performed in the future. Determined by discounting the future price of the work by a rate commensurate with the interest rate on the funds for the period before payment is required.

presolicitation conference
In U.S. federal government procurement, a meeting held by the contracting officer with prospective contractors as a preliminary step in negotiated acquisitions to develop or identify interested sources, request preliminary information based on a general description of the supplies or services involved, explain specifications and requirements, and aid prospective contractors in preparing proposals before making a large expenditure of effort, time, and money.

price
Monetary amount paid, received, or asked in exchange for supplies or services, which is expressed as a single item or unit of measure for the supplies or services.

price adjustment
Modification of the price as stated in the terms of a contract.

price analysis
Examination and evaluation of a prospective price, without performing cost analysis, by determining the reasonableness of the price offered with reference to similar items or services offered for sale in the marketplace.

price competition
In U.S. federal government procurement, competition in a procurement when offers are solicited and received from at least two responsible contractors capable of completely or partially satisfying requirements.

pricing arrangement
Basis agreed to by contractual parties for payment of amounts for specified performance generally through a specific type of contract, either cost-reimbursement or fixed-price.

primary failure

Failure of a system because of age, poor design, poor construction, or improper installation of a component.

prime contractor

Organization that is managerially, commercially, and technically capable of accepting a contract from a buyer and is responsible for coordinating activities of a number of subcontractors, integrating their deliverables, and managing risks to meet the buyer's requirements in terms of performance, cost, and schedule. "Prime" distinguishes the contract from any subcontract entered into between the prime contractor and a supplier or vendor called a subcontractor or between one subcontractor and another, lower-level subcontractor.

PRINCE2

See Projects in Controller Environments (Version 2).

principled negotiation

Negotiation approach with its primary objective the achievement of a win-win result.

priorities

Sequences desired regarding scheduling activities within previously imposed constraints.

priority rules

Formal methods, such as ratios, to rank items to determine which one should be next.

privatization

Process aimed at shifting functions and responsibilities, in whole or in part, from the government to the private sector.

privity of contract

Legal relationship and responsibilities between parties to the same contract.

probabilistic estimating
Method of estimating that generally uses three values to compute a statistically weighted estimate. *See also* Program Evaluation and Review Technique.

probability
(1) Likelihood of occurrence.
(2) Ratio of the number of chances that an event may or may not happen to the sum of the chances of both happening and not happening.

probability analysis
Risk quantification technique that entails specifying a probability distribution for each variable and then calculating values for situations in which any one or all of the variables are changed at the same time.

probability of acceptance
Percent of inspection lots expected to be accepted when the lots are subjected to a specific sampling plan.

problem definition
Process of distinguishing between causes and symptoms to determine the scope of effort to pursue on the project.

problem resolution
Interaction between two or more parties with the specific intent of finding a mutually acceptable solution to a technical or other problem that impacts project accomplishment.

problem solving
Also called confrontation. *See* conflict resolution.

problem/need statement/goal
Documentation that defines the problem to be resolved, reinforces the need to develop a solution, and describes the overall objectives of the customer.

procedures

(1) Step-by-step instructions on ways to perform a given task or activity; may be accompanied by a statement of purpose and policy for a task, examples of the results of a task, and so forth.
(2) Prescribed method to perform specified work.

process

(1) Series of actions, steps, or procedures leading to a result.
(2) High-level sequence or flow of tasks performed during production of a product or delivery of a service.

process adjustment

Immediate corrective or preventive action as a result of quality control measurements; generally handled according to procedures for overall change control.

process analysis

Structured approach used to identify and understand what an organization does; defines business processes and the necessary data used through specific diagramming techniques.

process average

Average percent of defective units or average number of defects per hundred units of product submitted by the manufacturer for original inspection.

process definition

Dividing a process into its component parts so that it may be described in detail.

process flowchart

Diagram showing how various elements of a system relate. *Also called* system flowchart.

process model

Approach to show how processes are linked together in a business unit.

process standard sheet

Tool for reducing work performance variation that contains managerial information, such as policies, rules, objectives, goals, and targets, and technical information, such as critical dimensions, work methods, measurement techniques, materials, equipment, process control methods, and specifications. Has sufficient detail and clarity to serve as a guide to job accomplishment so someone new can perform the job correctly the first time by following the standard.

procurement
Process of acquiring goods or services from outside the immediate project organization, beginning with determining the need for the supplies or services and ending with contract completion and closeout.

procurement audit
Structured review of the procurement process from procurement planning through contract administration to identify successes and failures. The lessons learned can be used later on the project or in other projects in the performing organization.

procurement considerations other than cost
Evaluation of staff and financial resources, facilities, performance record, responsiveness to contract terms and conditions, and a general willingness to perform the work as part of the evaluation process of a contractor's proposal.

procurement cost considerations
Assessment of the contractor's approach, realism, and reasonableness of cost, taking into account a forecast of economic factors affecting cost and cost risks used in the cost proposal.

procurement documents
Documents issued to prospective contractors when requesting bids or quotations for supply of goods or services.

procurement management plan
Document that describes the management of the procurement processes, from solicitation planning through contract closeout.

procurement performance evaluation
Comprehensive review of the original specification, statement of work, scope, and contract modifications for use in lessons learned to avoid similar problems in future procurements.

procurement planning
Process to determine what and when to procure.

procurement prequalification
Review of potential contractor's experience, past performance, capabilities, resources, and current work loads.

procurement ranking
Qualitative or quantitative evaluation of the capabilities and qualifications of prospective contractors for the purpose of selecting one or more of them to provide the proposed supplies or services.

procurement relationship with CWBS
Relationship of the supplies or services to be procured with the overall work and their interface with other project activities.

procurement response
Communications, positive or negative, from prospective contractors in response to the request to supply goods or services.

procurement source evaluation
Overall review of capabilities and ranking of prospective contractors for the purpose of requesting proposals or entering into negotiations for the award of the contract.

procurement strategy
Relationship of specific procurement actions to the project environment.

procurement technical considerations
Contractors' technical competency, understanding of the technical requirements, and capability to produce technically acceptable supplies or services.

procurement/buyer negotiations
See contract negotiations.

product
End result of a project or a specific task, activity, or process; either a tangible, physical product or a clearly specified event.

product analysis
Process to develop a better understanding of the product of the project. May include techniques such as systems engineering, value engineering, value analysis, function analysis, and quality function deployment.

product breakdown structure
Hierarchical structure used to decompose the product into constituent parts, as in a Bill of Materials.

product definition
Form, fit, and function of a deliverable or set of deliverables.

product description
Documentation delineating the product characteristics or service that the project was undertaken to create.

product development process
Structured, organized, and usually documented approach that organizations follow to design, develop, and introduce new products to the marketplace. Stages include, concept, selection, design, development, testing, availability, and maintenance.

product documentation
Written information about the product, which is a part of the final work product.

product liability
Responsibility of a producer or others to make restitution for loss related to personal injury, property damage, or other harm caused by a product.

product life cycle
Total period of time that a product exists in the marketplace, from concept to termination.

product quality review
Action taken by the buyer to determine that the quality of supplies or services accepted complies with specified requirements.

product scope
Features, functions, and characteristics to be included in a product.

product substitution
Delivery of a product that does not meet contract requirements.

production permit
Written authorization, before production or provision of a service, to depart from specified requirements for a specific quantity or a specific time. *Also called* deviation permit.

production readiness
System's readiness to proceed to the production phase.

production surveillance
Contract administration function used to determine contractor progress and identify any areas that might delay performance.

productivity
Measurement of criteria such as labor efficiency or equipment effectiveness against an established base.

product-oriented processes
Methods used to specify and create the project product; defined by the project life cycle but varying by application area.

product-oriented survey
Review and evaluation that determines the adequacy of the technical requirements relating to product quality and conformance to design specifications.

product-oriented WBS
See work breakdown structure.

profit
Amount realized after the total project costs (both direct and indirect) are deducted from the price.

profit and loss statement
Written summary of the revenues, costs, and expenses of a corporation during an accounting period.

profit objective
In U.S. federal government procurement, an amount that the contracting officer, in preparing to negotiate price based on cost analysis, concludes is the appropriate negotiated profit or fee for the specific procurement.

profitability
Measure of the total project income compared to the total monies expended at any given period of time. Includes techniques such as economic value added, payout time period, return on investment, net present value, and discounted cash flow.

program
Group of related projects managed in a coordinated way to obtain benefits not available from managing the projects individually; may include an element of ongoing activities or tasks.

program budgeting
Aggregating income and expenditures by project or program, often in addition to aggregating by organizational unit or activity.

Program Evaluation and Review Technique (PERT)
Event-oriented, probability-based network analysis technique used to estimate project duration when there is a high degree of uncertainty with the individual activity duration estimates. PERT applies the critical path method to a weighted average duration estimate. The formula is as follows:

$$\frac{O + 4\,(ML) + P}{6},$$

where O = optimistic time, ML = most likely time, and P = pessimistic time.

program management
Management of a related series of projects over a period of time, to accomplish broad goals to which the individual projects contribute.

program management office (PMO)
Organizational entity established to complete a number of projects that collectively satisfy a strategic or tactical organizational objective, usually headed by a program manager and staffed by professionals from various disciplines. When implementing a program management office, it is not uncommon for the staff, including the project managers, to report directly to the program manager in a supervisor-employee relationship. However, not all organizations adopt this specific approach, opting instead for a matrix form of organization.

program manager
Individual typically responsible for a number of related projects, each with its own project manager.

program office
See program management office.

progress payments
Interim payments for work according to contract terms that may be tied to specified performance milestones, a particular stage of completion of the project, or costs incurred.

progress reporting
Production of status reports that describe on a regular basis what the project team has accomplished.

progress trend
Indication of whether the progress rate of a task or project is increasing, decreasing, or remaining the same during a specific time period.

project
Temporary undertaking to create a unique product or service with a defined start and end point and specific objectives that, when attained, signify completion.

project accounting
Process of identifying, collecting, measuring, recording, and communicating actual project cost data.

project archives
Complete set of indexed project records; any project-specific or historical databases containing information about a project or group of projects.

project audit
Structured, formal review of a project, at any time in the project life cycle, to assess progress performance relative to time, cost, and technical objectives; typically conducted by a third party.

project baseline
Project management frame of reference established based on the detailed project plan and incorporating the project's cost, schedule, and quality objectives to serve as the basis for measuring progress, comparing planned and actual events and expenditures, and identifying and executing changes to the project's scope of work.

project breakdown structure (PBS)
Similar to the WBS but used in some application areas when the term WBS is incorrectly used to refer to a Bill of Materials.

project budget
Amount and distribution of funds allocated to a project.

project business case
Document containing the analysis and results of business assessments providing the justification to pursue a project opportunity.

project calendar
Calendar identifying the specific work periods during the project life cycle when resources will be consumed.

project charter
Document issued by senior management that gives the project manager authority to apply organizational resources to project activities and formally recognizes the existence of a project. Includes a description of the business need that the project was undertaken to address and a description of the product or service to be delivered by the project.

project closeout
Process to provide for project acceptance by the project sponsor, completion of various project records, final revision and issue of documentation to reflect the "as-built" condition, and retention of essential project documentation.

project communications management
Part of project management that includes the processes needed to ensure proper collection, dissemination, storage, and disposition of project information. Consists of communication planning, information distribution, performance reporting, and administrative closure.

project control
Activities associated with making decisions about present and future project activities. Usually based on the identification and collection of project performance information with the intent of ensuring successful project completion.

project coordinator

In some project organizational structures, an individual who reports to a higher-level manager in the organization (for example, at the CEO staff level), has the authority to assign work to individuals in various functional organizations, and shares authority and resources with functional managers.

project cost estimate

Sum total of all costs required to complete a project. In most organizations, the cost of maintaining and decommissioning the product or service created by the project is not included in this estimate. *See also* cost estimate.

project cost management

Part of project management that includes the processes required to ensure that the project is completed within an approved budget. Consists of resource planning, cost estimating, cost budgeting, and cost control.

project cost system

Cost accounting system that includes ledgers, asset records, liabilities, write-offs, taxes, depreciation expense, raw materials, prepaid expenses, salaries, and so on for the project.

project definition worksheet

Generic name used to identify any number of tools or templates that capture important project information to ensure that the project team addresses, and agrees upon, key project elements. Such elements include background and summary, goals and key deliverables, milestones, assumptions, risks, cost estimates, legal issues, or other relevant information.

project duration

Elapsed time from the project start date to the project finish date.

project environment

(1) Combined internal and external forces, both individual and collective, that assist or restrict attainment of the project objectives. These forces may be either business or project

related or may be a result of political, economic, technological, or regulatory conditions.

(2) Circumstances, objects, or conditions by which project team members are surrounded.

(3) Everything outside the project that delivers input or receives output from the project.

(4) Cultural, political, financial, moral, and ethical characteristics that impact how projects are completed.

project evaluation

Periodic examination of a project to determine whether the objectives are being met. Conducted at regular intervals, such as the beginning or end of a major phase. May result in redirection of the project with decisions to change the scope, time, or cost baselines, for example, or terminate the project. *See also* control gate.

project execution

See implementation phase.

project expeditor

In some project organizational structures, an individual who is a staff assistant to an executive who has the ultimate responsibility for the project. The project expeditor assumes the day-to-day responsibilities of the project manager and has authority over resources within his or her executive's department but not over resources from other departments.

project finish date

Latest calendar finish date of all activities on the project, based on network or resource allocation process calculations.

project goals

Milestones that lead to the completion of project work packages.

project human resource management

Part of project management that includes the processes necessary to ensure effective use of the people involved with the project; consists of organizational planning, staff acquisition, and team development.

project initiation
See initiation.

project integration
Process of bringing together diverse organizations, groups, parts, or activities to form a cohesive whole to successfully achieve project objectives.

project integration management
Part of project management that includes the processes required to ensure that the various project elements are coordinated effectively. Consists of project plan development, project plan execution, and overall change control.

project investment cost
Aggregation of all the project cost elements (capital and operating) as defined by an agreed-upon scope of work. An attempt is made to estimate the final financial outcome of a future investment program even though all the project parameters are not known.

project justification
Use of the business need or purpose that the project was undertaken to address to provide the basis for evaluating future investment trade-offs.

project leader
(1) Term generally synonymous with "project manager" but used more widely in Europe than elsewhere.
(2) Term preferred over "project manager" by some organizations because it more accurately reflects the leadership skills, in addition to the management competencies, required of the person in charge of a project.

project life cycle
Collection of generally sequential project phases whose specific name and number are determined by the organization or organizations involved in the project. Generally includes the

major steps involved in conceptualizing, designing, developing, and putting into operation (but not operating or disposing of) the project's technical performance deliverables.

project life-cycle cost

The sum total of all costs associated with the initiation, design, development, execution, and closeout of a project.

project management (PM)

Application of knowledge, skills, tools, and techniques to project activities to meet or exceed stakeholder needs and expectations from a project.

project management body of knowledge (PMBOK®)

Totality of knowledge within the project management profession. As in other professions, such as law, medicine, and accounting, the body of knowledge rests with the practitioners and academics involved in its application and advancement. The PMBOK® includes practices that have been widely applied and proven, as well as innovative and advanced practices with more limited use and application.

project management controls

Processes or procedures designed to ensure that project performance information is collected, analyzed, and reviewed by appropriate stakeholders and used to decide any course of action to achieve the project's objectives. Examples include time tracking, scope change requests, and control gates.

project management information system (PMIS)

(1) Systems, activities, and data that allow information flow in a project; frequently automated.
(2) Tools and techniques used to gather, integrate, and distribute output of the other project management processes.

Project Management Institute (PMI®), Inc.

International, nonprofit professional association dedicated to advancing the discipline of project management and state-of-the-art project management practices. *See also* project management professional.

project management methodology
Highly detailed description of the procedures to be followed in a project life cycle. Often includes forms, charts, checklists, and templates to ensure structure and consistency.

project management office
See project office.

project management portal
Web site, usually developed for commercial gain, that provides services, information, and references on project management. *See also* portal.

project management processes
Series of actions that describe and organize the work of the project.

project management professional (PMP®)
Professional certification awarded by the Project Management Institute to individuals who have met the established minimum requirements in knowledge, education, experience, and service in the discipline of project management.

project management software
Specific computer applications designed to aid in planning and controlling project costs and schedules.

project management team
Members of the project team who are directly involved in project management activities.

project manager
Individual responsible for managing the overall project and its deliverables. Acts as the customer's single point of contact for the project. Controls planning and execution of the project's activities and resources to ensure that established cost, time, and quality goals are met.

project metrics
Measurable criteria that indicates the overall status or performance of a project, program, or project management

practice. Can be technical, administrative, or management in nature, the data for which are collected regularly. Viewed by the organization as being necessary to gauge performance and make adjustments to processes and procedures. May include schedule performance, cost data, defect levels, customer satisfaction, employee morale, time-to-market performance, and so on.

project network diagram

Graphical depiction of the logical relationships between and among project activities.

project objectives

(1) Identified, expected results and benefits involved in successfully completing the project.
(2) Quantifiable criteria that must be met for the project to be considered successful.
(3) Project scope expressed in terms of output, required resources, and schedule.

project office

(1) Organizational entity established to assist project managers throughout the organization in implementing project management principles, practices, methodologies, tools, and techniques. In most implementations, the project office is a support function and is not responsible for project execution. Its main objective is implementing an effective project management practice throughout the organization. *Also called* a center of excellence *or* center of expertise.
(2) Organizational entity established to complete a specific project or series of projects, usually headed by a project manager.

project organization

Structure or arrangement of project participants.

project personnel

Members of the project team directly employed on a project.

project phase
Collection of logically related project activities, usually resulting in the completion of a major deliverable. Collectively, the project phases compose the project life cycle.

project plan
Formal, approved document, in summarized or detailed form, used to guide both project execution and control. Documents planning assumptions and decisions, facilitates communication among stakeholders, and documents approved scope, cost, and schedule baselines.

project plan development
Compilation of the results of all the other planning processes into a consistent, complete document.

project plan execution
Completion of the project plan by performing the activities described therein.

project planning
(1) Developing and maintaining the project plan; identifying the project objectives, activities needed to complete the project, and resources and quantities required to carry out each activity or task within the project.
(2) Approach to determine how to begin, sustain, and end a project.

project politics
Actions taken by a project manager or other stakeholder to cause a group of people with different interests to work toward a common goal.

project portfolio
Collection of projects to be managed concurrently; each project may be related to or independent of each other but falls under a single management umbrella.

project procurement management
Part of project management that includes the processes required to acquire supplies and services from outside the

performing organization. Consists of procurement planning, solicitation planning, solicitation, source selection, contract administration, and contract closeout.

project quality management
Part of project management that consists of processes required to ensure that the project will satisfy its objectives. Includes quality planning, quality assurance, and quality control.

project quality system
Organizational structure, responsibilities, procedures, processes, and resources needed to implement project quality management.

project records
Collection of correspondence, reports, memoranda, and documents describing the project. May be in hard copy or electronic form.

project recovery
Process of identifying, executing, monitoring, and controlling specific actions or alternatives to reduce or eliminate the significant variances relative to project time, cost, and technical performance.

project reporting
Communicating information about project status and progress.

project requirements
See functional requirements and technical requirements.

project resources
See resources.

project review
Periodic monitoring of project activities and tasks.

project risk
(1) Cumulative effect of the probability of uncertain occurrences that may positively or negatively affect project objectives.

(2) Degree of exposure to negative events and their probable consequences (opposite of opportunity). Characterized by three factors: risk event, risk probability, and amount at stake.

project risk management
That part of project management that includes the processes involved with identifying, analyzing, and responding to project risk; consists of risk identification, risk quantification, risk response development, and risk response control.

project risk manager
Person on the project team responsible for preparing and tracking a risk management plan and for integrating risk management issues into project planning and execution.

project schedule
Planned dates to perform activities and meet milestones.

project scope
All the work required to deliver a project's product or service with the specified features and functions.

project scope management
Part of project management that includes the processes required to ensure that the project includes all the work required, and only the work required, to successfully complete the project; consists of initiation, scope planning, scope definition, scope verification, and scope change control.

project segments
Subdivisions of the project expressed as manageable components.

project selection methods
Techniques, practices, or procedures used to select a project or group of projects that best supports the organization's objectives. Divided into two broad categories: (1) benefit measurement methods—comparative approaches, scoring models, benefit contribution assessments, and economic models—and (2) constrained optimization methods—

mathematical models using linear, nonlinear, dynamic, integer, and multiobjective programming algorithms.

project services
Expertise or labor needed to implement a project not available within the project manager's organization.

project sponsor
Person in an organization whose support and approval is required for a project to start and continue.

project stakeholder
Individual or organization who is actively involved in the project or whose interests may be affected, either positively or negatively, as a result of project execution or successful project completion. *Also sometimes called* party-at-interest.

project strategy
Plan with policies to provide general direction of how resources will be used to accomplish project goals and objectives.

project summary WBS
Special-purpose WBS that displays only the higher levels of the project WBS; used primarily for reporting to senior management or the customer.

project team
Group of people with complementary skills, a common purpose, shared goals, and mutual accountability who share responsibility for accomplishing project goals and who report either full or part time to the project manager.

project team roles
Identified authority, accountability, and responsibility of project team members individually and as a whole.

project termination
See project closeout.

project time management
Part of project management that includes processes required to ensure that the project is completed on time; consists of activity definition, activity sequencing, activity duration estimating, schedule development, and schedule control.

project WBS
See work breakdown structure.

project-based organization
Organization that derives its revenue primarily from performing projects for others.

projection
Estimate of future performance based on the review of historical information, present situation, and future outlook.

projectitis
Inappropriately intense loyalty to the project.

projectized organization
Organizational structure in which resources are assigned full time to the project manager, who has complete authority to assign priorities and direct the work of people on the project.

Projects in Controlled Environments (Version 2) (PRINCE 2)
Project management method covering the organization, management, and control of projects. First developed (in 1989) by the Central Computer and Telecommunications Agency as a United Kingdom government standard for information technology project management. More generic than the original method in that it focuses on a generic, best practice approach to project management.

promotional management style
Management approach in which the project manager encourages team members to realize their full potential, cultivates team spirit, and lets team members know that good work will be rewarded.

proof of concept
Evidence to support acceptance of a proposed solution.

proposal
(1) Procurement document prepared by the contractor to describe the contractor's ability and willingness to provide the requested product according to the requirements of the relevant solicitation document.
(2) Offer submitted by a contractor to enter into a contract, contract modification, or termination settlement. *See also* bid *and* quotation.

proposal project plan
Plan issued early in a project that may be part of the contractor's proposal and contains key analysis, procurement, and implementation milestones; historical data; and any client-supplied information. Sometimes presented in bar or Gantt chart form or as a summary level network, supported with narrative explanations and used for inquiry and contract negotiations.

protest
Written objection, submitted by an interested party, to a solicitation for offers or to the award or proposed award of a contract.

prototype
Small or full-scale, and usually functioning, form of a newly developed product, which is used to evaluate the product design.

provision
Written term or condition used only in solicitations and applying before contract award; distinguished from clauses, which are terms and conditions in contracts.

public relations
Activity designed to improve the environment in which a project organization operates with the aim of improving project

performance or otherwise promoting the goals and objectives of the project.

public-private partnership

Contractual arrangement, sometimes referred to as a joint venture, between public- and private-sector partners. Can include a variety of activities that involve the private sector in the development, financing, ownership, and operation of a public facility or service. Typically includes infrastructure projects or facilities. In such a partnership, public and private resources are pooled and responsibilities divided so that the partners' efforts complement one another. Typically, each partner shares in income resulting from the partnership in direct proportion to the partner's investment. Such a venture, although a contractual arrangement, differs from typical service contracting in that the private-sector partner usually makes a substantial cash, at-risk, equity investment in the project, and the public sector gains access to new revenue or new delivery capacity without having to pay the private-sector partner.

punch list

List prepared when the project is almost completed to show the items of work remaining to fulfill the project scope.

punitive damages

Monetary compensation, over and above actual damages, sought by a buyer to punish a seller for nonperformance or other wrongful acts.

purchase

Acquisition of items, mostly off-the-shelf or catalog, manufactured outside the purchaser's premises.

purchase description

Description of the essential physical characteristics and functions necessary to meet requirements.

purchase order

Offer to buy certain supplies, services, or construction from sources based on specified terms and conditions.

pure risk

See insurable risk.

purse-string authority

Influence based on the amount of control an individual has over the money used to carry out the project.

Q

QA

See quality assurance.

QAR

See quality assurance representative.

QC

See quality control.

qualified bidders list

List of contractors who have had their products examined and tested and who have satisfied all applicable qualification requirements for the product.

qualified manufacturers list

List of manufacturers who have had their products examined and tested and who have satisfied all applicable qualification requirements for the product.

qualified product

Product examined, tested, and qualified for inclusion on an applicable qualified products list.

qualified products list

List of products that the buyer has determined will satisfy project requirements, with accompanying names and addresses of the manufacturers or distributors and appropriate product identification and test reference data.

qualified sellers list

List or files of prospective contractors, including information on their relevant experience and other characteristics.

qualitative risk assessment

Non-numeric description of a risk, including the likelihood that it will occur, its impact, the methods for containing the impact, possible fallback or recovery measures, and ownership data.

quality

(1) Total characteristics of an entity or item that affect its ability to satisfy stated or implied needs.
(2) Conformance to requirements or specifications.
(3) Fitness for use.

quality assurance (QA)

(1) Process of regularly evaluating overall project performance to provide confidence that the project will satisfy relevant quality standards.
(2) Organizational unit responsible for quality assurance efforts.

quality assurance representative (QAR)

In U.S. federal government procurement, an individual, located at a contractor's facility, who is responsible for the government's procurement quality assurance function.

quality audit

Structured review of quality management activities to identify lessons learned and improve performance of the project or other projects within the organization.

quality circles

Small groups of employees who meet regularly to improve the process, product, or service of their organization. Key characteristic: they do not include any management representatives.

quality conformance inspection

Examinations and tests performed on items or services to determine conformance with specified requirements.

quality control (QC)

(1) Monitoring of specific project results to determine whether they comply with relevant quality standards and identification of ways to eliminate causes of unsatisfactory performance. (2) Organizational unit with responsibility for quality control efforts.

quality control measurements

Results of quality control testing and measures presented in a form for comparison and analysis.

quality council

Group of individuals, typically comprising senior managers, that is responsible for coordinating the quality program in an organization.

quality evaluation

Technical process of gathering measured variables or counted data for decision making in a quality process review.

quality function deployment

Process used to provide better product definition and product development and to help a design team define, design, manufacture, and deliver a product or service that meets or exceeds customer needs. Strives to ensure that the customer's definition of product or service specifications is used, work is performed by strong cross-functional teams, and the major phases of product development are linked.

quality gate

Predefined completion criterion for a task, including audits, walk-throughs, and inspections that provide an assessment of progress, processes used, and project products to be delivered.

quality improvement

Action taken to increase the effectiveness and efficiency of the project to provide added benefits to project stakeholders.

quality loop
Conceptual model of interacting activities that influence the quality of a product or service in various stages ranging from needs identification to assessment of whether the needs have been satisfied. *Also called* quality spiral.

quality management
(1) Planning, organizing, staffing, coordinating, directing, and controlling activities of management with the objective of achieving the required quality.
(2) Overall management function involved in determining and implementing quality policy.

quality management plan
Document that describes how the project management team will implement its quality policy. The quality management plan becomes part of the overall project plan and incorporates quality control, quality assurance, and project quality improvement procedures.

quality philosophy
Established quality policies and procedures that are used to guide work throughout the organization and serve as the basis for performing project work.

quality planning
Identifying the specific quality standards that are relevant to the project and determining how to satisfy them.

quality policy
Overall intentions and directions of the organization concerning quality, as formally expressed by top management.

quality predictor
Measure for estimating the likelihood of conforming to the specifications identified to produce a product or deliver a service.

quality process review
Technical process of using data to determine how the actual project results compare with the quality specifications or

requirements. If deviations occur, the review may result in changes in the project design, development, use, and so on, depending on the decisions of the client, involved stakeholders, and project team.

quality product
A product that meets or exceeds the customer's expectations.

quality program requirement
Requirement to establish and maintain a quality program according to the MIL-Q-9858 specification that states that the program shall ensure adequate quality throughout all areas of contract performance, for example, design, development, fabrication, processing, assembly, inspection, test, maintenance, packaging, shipping, storage, and site installation.

quality risk
Failure to complete tasks to the required level of technical or quality performance.

quality spiral
See quality loop.

quality surveillance
Ongoing monitoring and verification of the status of procedures, methods, conditions, processes, products, and services and the analysis of records related to stated requirements to ensure that specified quality requirements are being met.

quality system
(1) Organizational structure, responsibilities, procedures, processes, and resources to implement quality management.
(2) Procedures, processes, people, management, tools, and facilities involved in ensuring that quality is built into a product or service.

quality system review
Formal evaluation by top management of the status and adequacy of the quality system in relation to the organization's quality policy and other relevant objectives.

quantitative risk assessment
Numeric analysis of risk estimates including probability of occurrence to forecast the project's schedule and costs using probabilistic data and other identified uncertainties to determine likely outcomes.

quotation
Procurement document generally used when the award decision will be price driven; does not constitute a binding offer in U.S. federal government procurements. *See also* bid *and* proposal.

R

RAM
See responsibility assignment matrix.

random cause
Indeterminable reason that precipitates a special event, that is, one that is outside the control limits.

random sampling
Sampling method in which each unit of the population has an equal chance of being selected.

range estimating
Applying probabilistic modeling to cost estimates as an adjunct to traditional estimating, not as a substitute for it. Includes identifying the mathematical probability of a cost overrun, amount of financial exposure, risks and opportunities ranked according to bottom-line importance, and contingency required for a given level of confidence. Can also be used in schedule estimating.

rapid prototyping

Building a sample product from preliminary system requirements, and showing the customer the prototype of the deliverable to obtain its reactions and input. *See also* application prototyping.

Rayleigh curve

Roughly bell-shaped curve that represents the buildup and decline of staff power, effort, or cost, followed by a long trail representing staff power, effort, or cost devoted to enhancement or maintenance.

RBS

See resource breakdown structure.

RDU

See remaining duration.

real property

Land and whatever is erected on it, growing on it, or affixed to it.

reasonableness of cost

(1) Cost of an item or service not exceeding that which would be incurred by someone conducting a competitive business.
(2) Element in the determination of whether a cost is allowable.

rebaselining

Establishing a new project baseline because of sweeping or significant changes in the project scope. Must be approved by all parties.

record retention

Period of time that records are kept for reference after contract or project closeout.

records management

Procedures established by an organization to identify, index, archive, and distribute all documentation associated with the project.

recovery
  (1) Act of correcting problems on a current project to improve its chances of success.
  (2) Restoration of computing facilities after a system failure.

recovery schedule
  Special schedule showing efforts to take to recover time lost on the project, as compared to the master schedule.

recruitment practices
  Policies, guidelines, or procedures concerning initial assignment of staff.

recurring cost
  Production cost, such as labor and materials, that varies with the quantity produced, as distinguished from nonrecurring cost.

red team
  Independent peer-level review team usually used to provide feedback on proposals but useful for any documentation and presentation material.

reduced inspection
  Inspection under a sampling plan using the same quality level as that in a normal inspection but requiring a smaller sample.

reference base
  Source of detailed cost information within a function or organization from which estimates and budgets may, in part, be established for work relating to that function. For example, a piecemeal reference base of US$10 per widget may be used to establish a US$10,000 apportioned cost account budget for an activity to develop 1,000 widgets.

referent authority
  Influence based on an individual's referring to a higher power as supporting his or her position or recommendation. ("The boss and I think this is a good idea.")

refinement

Rework, redefinition, or modification of the logic or data that may have been already developed as part of the project planning process to more accurately describe milestones, constraints, and priorities.

regression analysis

Statistical technique used to establish and graphically depict the relationship of a dependent variable to one or more independent variables.

regulation

Written description of the product, process, or service characteristics and the needed compliance with applicable administrative provisions.

reimbursement

Payment to a seller, employee, or other party for incurred expenses in project performance or any aspect of work associated with an organization.

rejection number

Minimum number of defects or defective units in a sample that will cause rejection of the entire lot represented by the sample.

release

Agreement by a contracting party that the other party will not be liable for any future claims.

release claims

Certificate that releases and holds the customer harmless from any future claims by the contractor.

reliability

Ability of an item to perform a required function under stated conditions for a stated period of time.

reliability assurance

Actions necessary to provide adequate confidence that the material conforms to established reliability requirements.

remaining available resources
Difference between the resource availability pool and scheduled resource requirements. Computed during the resource allocation process.

remaining duration (RDU)
Time required to complete an activity.

remaining float (RF)
Difference between the early finish and the late finish date.

remedy
Right of a contracting party when the other party does not fulfill its contractual obligations.

reporting
Communicating information regarding project status and progress.

representative sample
Sample in which the number of units selected in proportion to the size of sublots, sub-batches, or parts of the lot or batch are identified by some rational criterion and selected at random.

request for proposals (RFP)
Type of bid document used to solicit proposals from prospective contractors for products or services. Used when items or services are of a complex nature and assumes that negotiation will take place between the buyer and the contractor.

request for quotations (RFQ)
Similar to request for proposals but generally with a lower monetary amount involved in the procurement. Used to solicit proposals from prospective contractors for standard products or services such that negotiation may not be required.

requirements analysis
Process of evaluating the customer's stated needs and validating them against specific organizational requirements and plans.

requirements traceability

Process of understanding, documenting, approving, and auditing the relationships between a system's components and functions and the requirements from which the system was developed. Each function and component of a system should be directly traceable to a requirement identified by a user, client, customer, or stakeholder.

reschedule

Change logic, duration, or dates of an existing schedule because of corrective actions or externally imposed conditions.

rescission

Release of a party from all obligations under a contract.

reserve

Money or time provided for in the project plan to mitigate cost, schedule, or performance risk. *See also* management reserve *and* contingency reserve.

residual value

Value of a fixed asset after depreciation charges have been subtracted from its original cost.

resource allocation

Process of assigning resources to the activities in a network while recognizing any resource constraints and requirements; adjusting activity level start and finish dates to conform to resource availability and use.

resource availability date

Calendar date when a given resource or resource pool becomes available.

resource availability pool

Number of resources available for a given allocation period.

resource breakdown structure (RBS)

Variation of the organizational breakdown structure used to show which work elements are assigned to individuals.

resource calendar
Calendar denoting when a resource or resource pool is available for work on a project.

resource code
Method used to identify a given resource type.

resource conflict
Situation that arises because of the allocation of one resource to more than one task.

resource description
Actual name or way to identify a resource code.

resource Gantt chart
Variation of the horizontal bar Gantt chart used to show how resources are allocated over time, task by task, and how the resources will be distributed throughout the life of the project. Used to track and plan resource allocations and to identify when resources are overallocated.

resource histogram
Vertical bar chart used to show resource consumption by time period. *Also called* resource loading chart.

resource leveling
(1) Practicing a form of network analysis in which scheduling decisions (start and finish dates) are driven by resource management issues (such as limited resource availability or changes in resource levels).
(2) Evening out the peaks and valleys of resource requirements so that a fixed amount of resources can be used over time.
(3) Ensuring that a resource is maximized but not used beyond its limitations.

resource loading
Designating the amount and type of resources to be assigned to a specific activity in a certain time period.

resource loading chart
See resource histogram.

resource matrix
Structure used to allocate types of resources to tasks by listing the tasks in the WBS along the vertical axis and the resources required along the horizontal axis. Differs from a responsibility assignment matrix in that assignments of specific individuals are typically not depicted.

resource plan
Document used to describe the number of resources needed to accomplish the project work and the steps necessary to obtain a resource.

resource planning
Process of determining resources (people, equipment, materials) needed in specific quantities, and during specific time periods, to perform project activities.

resource pool
Collection of human and material resources that may be used concurrently on several projects.

resource pool description
Information about the resources (people, equipment, material) that are potentially available for use on the project.

resource rate
Unit rate (such as staff cost per hour or bulk material cost per cubic meter) for each resource needed to calculate project costs.

resource requirements
Output of the resource planning process, which describes the types and quantities of resources required for each element of the WBS. Resources are then obtained through staff acquisition or procurement.

resource selection
Process of choosing the type, amount, and sources of resources necessary to accomplish a work effort.

resource spreadsheet

Tool used to show the number of resource units needed on the project, by type, at different periods of time. By adding all resource requirements for each time unit, the total resource requirements for the project by time period can be calculated. The output of this spreadsheet can also be displayed as a resource histogram.

resource-constrained scheduling

Special case of resource leveling where the start and finish dates of each activity are calculated based on the availability of a fixed quantity of resources.

resource-limited planning

Planning activities so that predetermined resource availability levels are not exceeded. Activities begin as soon as resources are available (subject to logic constraints) as required by the activity.

resource-limited schedule

Project schedule whose start and end dates for each activity have been established on the availability of a fixed and finite set of human and material resources.

resources

People, equipment, or materials required or used to accomplish an activity. In certain applications, such things as "nonrainy days" are described as a resource.

response planning

Process of formulating project risk management strategies, including allocating responsibility to the project's various functional areas. May involve avoidance, acceptance, mitigation, and the use of certain tools and techniques such as deflection and contingency planning.

response system

Ongoing process during the project to monitor, review, and update any project risks and make necessary adjustments.

responsibility

(1) Obligation of an individual or group to perform assignments effectively.

(2) Status of a prospective contractor that determines whether it is eligible for contract award.

responsibility assignment matrix (RAM)

Structure used to relate the WBS to individual resources to ensure that each element of the project's scope of work is assigned to an individual. A high-level RAM defines which group or unit is responsible for each WBS element; a low-level RAM assigns roles and responsibilities for specific activities to particular people. *Also called* accountability matrix. *See also* resource matrix.

responsibility chart

See responsibility assignment matrix.

responsibility matrix

See responsibility assignment matrix.

resubmitted lot

Lot that has been either rejected or subjected to examination or testing to remove all defective units; it may later be reworked or replaced and submitted again for acceptance.

retainage

Withholding of a portion of a contract payment until contract completion to ensure full performance of the contract terms.

return on equity (ROE)

Amount, usually expressed as a percentage, earned on a company's common stock investment for a given period of time.

return on invested capital

See return on investment.

return on investment (ROI)
Amount of gain, expressed as a percentage, earned on an organization's total capital; calculated by dividing total capital into earnings before interest, taxes, and dividends.

return on sales (ROS)
Measure of operational efficiency that varies widely from industry to industry. ROS is the net pretax profits as a percentage of net sales.

revenue
Amount of money earned as a result of completing a project, selling a product, or providing a service.

reverse engineering
Developing design specifications by inspection and analysis of an existing product.

reverse scheduling
Method in which the project completion date is fixed and task duration and dependency information is used to compute the corresponding project start date.

review
Critical examination to determine suitability or accuracy. *See also* phase-end review.

revision
Special category of a schedule update in which changes are made to the start and finish dates in the approved project schedule; generally, dates are revised only because of scope changes. In some cases, rebaselining is then required. *See also* rebaselining.

reward and recognition system
Formal management actions to promote or reinforce desired behavior. To be effective, such a system should make the link between performance and reward clear, explicit, and achievable and should consider individual differences (for example, what is considered a highly motivating reward by one person may be seen as uninteresting by another).

reward authority

Influence derived from an individual's being able to provide positive reinforcement for desired behavior. For example, a project manager provides recognition and bonuses to top performers, further motivating them to project success.

rework

Action taken to ensure that a defective or nonconforming item complies with requirements or specifications.

RF

See remaining float.

RFP

See request for proposals.

RFQ

See request for quotations.

risk

See project risk.

risk acceptance

See acceptance.

risk allowance

Time or money budgeted to cover uncertainties because of inaccuracies in deterministic estimates or the occurrence of risk events. *See also* contingency reserve *and* management reserve.

risk analysis

Analysis of the probability that certain undesirable and beneficial events will occur and their impact on attaining project objectives. *See also* risk assessment.

risk and opportunity assessment model (ROAM)

Specific technique developed by ESI International to quantify the identified risks and opportunities associated with a particular project to help decide whether the project should be undertaken.

risk appraisal
Work involved in identifying and assessing risk.

risk assessment
(1) Review, examination, and judgment to see whether the identified risks are acceptable according to proposed actions. (2) Identification and quantification of project risks to ensure that they are understood and can be prioritized. *Also called* risk evaluation.

risk avoidance
See avoidance.

risk budget
Cost and schedule allowance that is held in reserve and spent only if uncertainties or risks occur. A combination of contingency and management reserves.

risk consequence
See impact.

risk contingency
See contingency.

risk database
Database for risks associated with a project.

risk deflection
See deflection.

risk description
Documentation of the risk element to identify the boundaries of the risk.

risk evaluation
See risk assessment.

risk event
Discrete occurrence that may affect a project, positively or negatively. *See also* project risk.

risk event status
(1) Measure of importance of a risk event. Also referred to as criterion value or ranking.
(2) Probability and impact of a risk as of the data date.

risk exposure
(1) Impact value of a risk multiplied by its probability of occurring.
(2) Loss provision made for a risk; requires that a sufficient number of situations in which this risk could occur have been analyzed.

risk factor
Risk event, risk probability, or amount at stake.

risk identification
Determining the risk events that are likely to affect the project and classifying them according to their cause or source.

risk management
See project risk management.

risk management plan
Documentation of the procedures to be used to manage risk during the life of a project and the parties responsible for managing various areas of risk. Includes procedures for performing risk identification and quantification, planning risk response, implementing contingency plans, allocating reserves, and documenting results.

risk management strategy
Formal statement of how risk management will be implemented for a project, what resources will be used, and, if applicable, what roles subcontractors will play.

risk mitigation
See mitigation.

risk portfolio
Risk data assembled and collated for project management.

risk prioritizing
Filtering, grouping, and ranking risks following assessment.

risk probability
Assessment of the likelihood that a risk event will occur.

risk quantification
Evaluation of the probability of a risk event's occurring and of its effect.

risk response control
Process of implementing risk strategies, documenting risk, and responding to changes in risk during the life of the project.

risk response development
Identification of specific actions to maximize the occurrence of opportunities and minimize the occurrence of specific risks in a project.

risk summary
Description of each risk factor, including its effect, ownership, and recommendations for response development.

risk symptom
Indirect manifestation of an actual risk event, such as poor morale serving as an early warning signal of an impending schedule delay or cost overruns on early activities pointing to poor estimating. *Also called* risk trigger.

risk trigger
See risk symptom.

roadblock
Impediment to progress or obstruction that prevents people, teams, and organizations from meeting objectives.

ROAM
See risk and opportunity assessment model.

robust design

Design that is capable of properly performing its function under a wide range of conditions, including some anticipated level of customer misuse.

ROE

See return on equity.

ROI

See return on investment.

rolling wave budgeting

Budgeting approach in which a full-period projection is made using an unsupported, top-down budget at the beginning of the project. As time progresses, the top-down budget is replaced with a more detailed, bottom-up budget that extends 3 to 6 months into the near-term future. A top-down budget is then used again at the end of the project.

rolling wave planning

Progressive detailing of the project plan as necessary to control each subsequent project phase.

rollout

Widespread, phased introduction of a project's product or service into the organization.

ROS

See return on sales.

royalty

Payment made by one party to another for use of its intellectual assets, conveyances, leases, or inventions. Based on a percentage of profit, sales, production, or other criteria agreed to by the parties.

S

sample

One or more units of product selected from a lot or batch at random or according to an established sampling plan for quality control purposes. *See also* representative sample *and* biased sample.

sample frequency

Ratio of the number of units of product randomly selected for inspection to the number of units of product passing the inspection station.

sample plan

Documentation of the sample size or sizes to be used and the associated acceptance and rejection criteria.

sample plan, double

Type of sampling plan in which the decision to accept or reject the first sample leads to a decision to take a second sample. Inspection of a second sample then leads to a decision to accept or reject.

sample plan, multilevel, continuous

Type of sampling plan in which the inspection periods of 100 percent inspection and two or more levels of sampling inspection are alternated, and the sampling frequency is constant or may change as a result of the inspection.

sample plan, multiple

Type of sampling plan in which the decision to accept or reject an inspection lot may be reached when at least one sample from that inspection lot has been inspected and will always be reached when a designated number of samples has been inspected.

sample plan, sequential

Type of sampling plan in which the sample units are selected one at a time. After inspection of each unit, a decision is made to accept, reject, or continue inspection until the acceptance or rejection criteria are met. Sampling ends when the inspection results of the sample units determine that the acceptance or rejection decision can be made. Sample size is not fixed in advance and depends on actual inspection results.

sample plan, single
Type of sampling plan in which a decision to accept or reject an inspection lot is based on only one sample.

sample plan, single-level, continuous
Type of sampling plan in which the inspection periods of 100 percent inspection and sampling inspection are alternated, and the sampling rate remains constant.

sample size
Number of units of product in the sample selected for inspection.

sample unit
Unit of product selected to be part of a sample.

scalable model
Cost estimating model that works as well for a very large project as for a very small one.

scenario planning
Technique that allows decision-makers to explore the implications of several alternative future states thus avoiding the danger of single-point forecasts. Conducted in a nonthreatening group setting, participants express beliefs, challenge assumptions, and alter their viewpoints to ultimately arrive at a strategic direction that is flexible and will remain so as actual events unfold.

schedule
Time-sequenced plan of activities or tasks used to direct and control project execution. Usually shown as a milestone chart, Gantt or other bar chart, or tabular listing of dates.

schedule analysis
See network analysis.

schedule baseline

Approved project schedule that serves as the basis for measuring and reporting schedule performance.

schedule change control system

Procedures followed to change the schedule. Includes paperwork, tracking systems, and approval levels needed to authorize changes.

schedule compression

See duration compression.

schedule control

Management of project schedule changes.

schedule development

Analysis of activity sequences, activity durations, and resource requirements to prepare the project schedule.

schedule management plan

Document used to define management of schedule changes; a subsidiary element of the overall project plan.

schedule performance index (SPI)

Ratio of work performed to work scheduled (BCWP/BCWS). The project is behind schedule if the SPI is less than one. *See also* earned value.

schedule refinement

Necessary rework, redefinition, or modification of the schedule logic or data developed during planning, which is based on activity on the project such as milestones, constraints, and priorities.

schedule revision

Changes to the scheduled start and finish dates in the approved project schedule.

schedule risk

Risk that jeopardizes completing the project according to the approved schedule.

schedule simulation

Use of the project network as a model of the project with the results used to quantify the risks of various schedule alternatives, project strategies, paths through the network, or individual activities. Most schedule simulations are based on some form of Monte Carlo analysis.

schedule update

Schedule revision to reflect the most current status of the project.

schedule variance (SV)

(1) Difference between the scheduled completion of an activity and its actual completion.
(2) In earned value, BCWP less BCWS; an SV of less than zero shows that project activity is behind schedule.

schedule work unit

Calendar time unit when work can be performed on an activity.

scheduled finish date

Point in time when work is scheduled to finish on an activity; normally, between the early and late finish dates. *Also called* planned finish date.

scheduled start date

Point in time when work is scheduled to start on an activity; normally, between the early and late start dates. *Also called* planned start date.

scheduling

(1) Fitting tasks into a logical timetable with detailed planning of work with respect to time.
(2) Determining when each item of preparation and execution must be performed.

scientific wild anatomical guess (SWAG)

Estimate of time or cost of completing a project or element of work based solely on the experience of the estimator. Typically done in haste, SWAG estimates are usually no more accurate than order-of-magnitude estimates.

scope
Sum of the products and services to be provided by the project.

scope baseline
See baseline.

scope baseline approval
Approval of the baseline by the appropriate authority (project sponsor or senior management).

scope change
Modification to the agreed-upon project scope as defined by the approved WBS.

scope change control
Process of (1) influencing the factors that cause scope changes to help ensure that the changes are beneficial, (2) determining that a scope change has occurred, and (3) managing the changes if and when they occur.

scope change control system
Procedures used to change the scope of the project, including paperwork, tracking systems, and approval levels needed to authorize changes.

scope constraint
Restriction affecting project scope.

scope cost
Estimated cost of performing the work as defined in the project scope statement.

scope creep
Gradual progressive increase of the project's scope such that it is not noticed by the project management team or the customer. Occurs when the customer identifies additional, sometimes minor, requirements that, when added together, may

collectively result in a significant scope change and cause cost and schedule overruns.

scope criteria
Standards or rules composed of parameters considered in project definition.

scope definition
Division of the major deliverables into smaller, more manageable components to (1) improve the accuracy of cost, time, and resource estimates; (2) define a baseline for performance measurement and control; and (3) facilitate clear responsibility assignments.

scope interfaces
Points of interaction between the project and its components or its respective environments.

scope management
See project scope management.

scope management plan
Document that describes the management of project scope, integration of any scope changes into the project, and identification and classification of scope changes.

scope of the contract
Work contemplated by the contractor and the buyer at the time of contract award.

scope of work
Description of the totality of work to be accomplished or resources to be supplied under a contract. *See also* statement of work.

scope planning
Developing a written scope statement that includes the project justification, major deliverables, project objectives, and criteria used to determine whether the project or phase has been successfully completed.

scope reporting
Process of periodically documenting project status in terms of cost as it affects financial status, schedule as it affects time-constraint status, and technical performance as it affects quality.

scope risks
Risks associated with scope or the need for "fixes" to achieve the required technical deliverables.

scope statement
Documented description of the project concerning its output, approach, and content. Used to provide a documented basis to help make future project decisions and to confirm or develop a common understanding of the project's scope by stakeholders.

scope verification
Process of ensuring that all identified project deliverables have been completed satisfactorily.

screening
Technique used to review, analyze, rank, and select the best alternative for the proposed action.

screening inspection
Inspection in which each item of product is inspected for designated characteristics, and defective items are removed.

screening system
Minimum performance requirements for one or more of the evaluation criteria used to select a contractor.

S-curve
Graphic display of cumulative costs, labor hours, or other quantities, plotted against time. The curve is flat at the beginning and end and steep in the middle. Generally describes a project that starts slowly, accelerates, and then tapers off.

sealed bidding

In U.S. federal government procurement, a contracting method that solicits submission of competitive bids through an invitation for bids followed by public opening of the bids and contract award to the responsive and responsible contractor.

second source

Alternative source for supply or service used to help foster competition.

secondary failure

System failure because of the use of a component in excessive conditions, such as heat or vibration.

secondary float

See free float.

secretive management style

Management approach in which the project manager is neither open nor outgoing in speech, activity, or purpose, to the detriment of the project.

self-inspection

Process in which the individual performing a task also conducts the measurement to ensure that requirements or specifications are met.

sensitivity analysis

Assessment of the impact that a change will have on the expected outcome of a process or project. Such change may involve modifying the value of one or more of the variables or assumptions used to predict the outcome.

service contract

Contract that directly engages the time and effort of a contractor to perform an identified task rather than to furnish a physical product.

service liability
Responsibility of a producer or others to make restitution for loss related to personal injury, property damage, or other harm caused by a service.

severance pay
Payment, in addition to regular salaries and wages, to workers whose employment is being involuntarily terminated.

shared leadership style
Management approach in which the project manager holds that leadership consists of many functions and that these can be shared among team members. Some common functions are time keeping, record keeping, planning, scheduling, and facilitating.

shareholder
Owner of one or more shares of a corporation usually evidenced by the holding of certificates or other formal documents.

shareholder manager style
Management approach in which little or no information input or exchange takes place within the team, but the team has the ultimate authority for the final decision.

shareholder value analysis
Process that attempts to demonstrate to shareholders how certain management decisions affect a company's ability to earn more than its total cost of capital. Used at both the corporate and individual business unit levels, this process provides such information to decision-makers as a framework for measuring the tradeoffs among reinvesting in existing businesses, investing in new businesses, and returning cash to stockholders.

short-term plan
(1) Short-term schedule showing detailed activities and responsibilities for a particular period (usually 4 to 8 weeks).

(2) Management technique often used "as needed" or in a critical area of the project.

should cost
Estimate of contract price that reflects reasonably achievable contractor economy and efficiency.

should-cost estimate
Estimate of the cost of a product or service used to assess the reasonableness of a prospective contractor's proposed cost.

significant variance
Difference between the plan and actual performance that jeopardizes the project objectives.

simulation
Technique used to emulate a process; usually conducted a number of times to understand the process better and to measure its outcomes under different policies.

single point of contact (SPOC)
See point of contact.

single source
One supplier from whom is procured the entire quantity of goods or services required even though other competitive suppliers are available.

situation analysis
Review process used to identify and define facts and variables that might influence a situation.

six sigma
Quality concept and aim developed by Motorola, Inc. and defined as a measure of goodness—the capability of a process to produce perfect work. Six sigma refers to the number of standard deviations from the average setting of a process to the tolerance limit, which in statistical terms translates to 3.4 defects per million opportunities for error.

slack
See float.

smoothing
See conflict resolution.

sociocultural barrier
Real or perceived inhibitor of communication, association, or equality among groups of people.

soft logic
See discretionary dependency.

software
Computer's set of instructions to carry out various applications and tasks.

Software Engineering Institute (SEI)
U.S. government Federally Funded Research and Development Center (FFRDC), operated by Carnegie-Mellon University in Pittsburgh, Pennsylvania, under contract to the U.S. Department of Defense (DOD). SEI's mission is to improve software engineering processes for the DOD. Has become well-known worldwide for its software Capability Maturity Model (CMM), used by software development professionals to improve the processes by which they develop application programs.

sole source
Only source known to be able to perform a contract or the one source among others that for a justifiable reason is considered to be the most advantageous for the purpose of contract award.

solicitation
(1) Obtaining quotations, bids, offers, or proposals as appropriate.
(2) Document sent to prospective contractors requesting the submission of offers or information.

solicitation planning
Documenting product or service requirements and identifying potential sources.

SOR
See statement of requirements.

source selection
Process of choosing from among potential contractors.

source selection procedures
Approaches used to maximize competition; minimize complexity of the solicitation, evaluation, and selection process; ensure impartial and comprehensive evaluation of proposals; and select the source whose proposal is most advantageous and realistic.

sources of risk
Categories of possible risk events that may affect the project positively or negatively. Descriptions of risk sources should include rough estimates of the probability that a risk event from that source will occur, the range of possible outcomes, the expected timing, and the anticipated frequency of risk events from the source.

SOW
See statement of work.

span of control
Number of individuals (direct reports) that a manager or project manager can effectively manage. The number will vary, but generally, a manager should have no more than ten direct reports. Once that number is exceeded, the organizational structure needs to be reviewed and changed. *See also* division of labor.

special cause variation
See special event.

special event
Variation in a product or delivery of a service that does not follow a normal distribution; event that falls outside the established control limits on a statistical process control chart.

specialist
Expert in a particular field who may be used as a resource for multiple projects in an organization.

specialty team structure
Organizational structure in which team members apply their special expertise across a number of tasks so that their skills can be used where and when appropriate.

specification
Description of the technical requirements for a material, product, or service, including the criteria for determining that the requirements have been met. Generally, three types of specifications are used in projects: performance, functional, and design.

specification control
System to ensure that project specifications are prepared in a uniform fashion and are changed only with proper authorization.

SPI
See schedule performance index.

spiral model
Progressive method of software development in which successive, more complete versions of the product are developed and verified only to be scrapped and replaced by a more complete and technically comprehensive version. This development approach usually involves close interaction and feedback with the ultimate end-user of the application program.

sponsor
Individual or group in the performing organization providing the financial resources, in cash or in kind, for the project.

staff acquisition

Process of obtaining the human resources needed to work on the project.

staffing management plan

Document that describes when and how human resources will become part of the project team and when they will return to their organizational units; may be a part of the overall project plan.

staffing requirements

Determination of what kinds of skills are needed from what types of individuals or groups, how many, and in what time frames; a subset of the overall resource requirements.

stage gate

See control gate.

stakeholder

See project stakeholder.

stakeholder analysis

Assessment of project stakeholder information needs and sources and development of reporting procedures to meet those needs.

stakeholder management

Action taken by the project manager or project team for curtailing stakeholder activities that would adversely affect the project.

standard

(1) Basis for uniformly measuring or specifying performance.
(2) Document used to prescribe a specific consensus solution to a repetitive design, operations, or maintenance situation.
(3) Document approved by a recognized body that provides for common and repeated use, rules, guidelines, or characteristics for products, processes, or services; however, compliance is not mandatory.

(4) Document that establishes engineering and technical limitations and applications of items, materials, processes, methods, designs, and engineering practices.

standard cost
(1) Cost computed with the use of pre-established methods.
(2) Goal or baseline cost used to expedite the process of costing transactions determined from historical experience or derived from the best available information.

standard operating procedure (SOP)
Detailed step-by-step procedure for repetitive operations.

standard procedure
Documented prescription that a certain type of work be done in the same way wherever it is performed.

standard wage rate
Normal or base salary of an employee before overtime or premium pay is computed.

standards method
Approach used in budgeting and measuring performance that requires that standards be established for the performance of the specific tasks; generally used in manufacturing.

start date
Point in time associated with an activity's start. Usually qualified by one of the following terms: actual, planned, estimated, scheduled, early, late, target, baseline, or current.

start-to-finish
Relationship in a precedence diagramming method network in which one activity must start before the successor activity can finish.

start-to-start
Relationship in a precedence diagramming method network in which one activity must start before the successor activity can start.

startup

Period after the date of initial operation, during which the unit is brought up to acceptable production capacity and quality. Often confused with the date of initial operation.

statement of requirements (SOR)

Type of statement of work in which the procurement item is presented as a problem to be solved, rather than a clearly specified product or service.

statement of work (SOW)

Narrative description of products or services to be supplied under contract that states the specifications or other minimum requirements; quantities; performance dates, times, and locations, if applicable; and quality requirements. Serves as the basis for the contractor's response and as a baseline against which the progress and subsequent contractual changes are measured during contract performance. *See also* statement of requirements.

statistical process control

Method used in quality control to monitor product and service quality. Based on the collection and analysis of data obtained during the manufacture of a product or the delivery of a service. Plotted on a graph. Helps identify whether the process is producing the results expected and helps pinpoint causes of special variation.

statistical sampling

Choosing part of a population of interest for inspection.

statistical sums

Sums used to calculate a range of total project costs from the cost estimates for individual work items to help quantify the relative risk of alternative project budgets or proposal prices.

status

Condition of the project at a specified point in time, relative to time, cost, or performance.

status report
(1) Description of where the project currently stands; part of the performance reporting process.
(2) Formal report on the input, issues, and actions resulting from a status meeting.

status review meeting
Regularly scheduled meeting held to exchange information about the project.

stochastic
Probabilistic; not deterministic.

stop work order
Formal request to stop work because of nonconformance, funding, or technical limitations.

storage quality control
Technical inspection of material received from vendors, which was not previously inspected at source and for which acceptance at destination is required.

straight-line method of depreciation
Method in which an equal amount of an asset's cost is considered an expense for each year of its useful life.

strategic design and implementation
Development and execution of a plan for meeting an organization's goals and objectives through the planned use of resources.

strategic partnership
Voluntary formation of a business relationship among or between independent organizations in support of a long-term strategy of mutual interest and benefits; typically based on a documented agreement of mutual cooperation.

strategic planning
Type of planning to establish the mission, objectives, goals, and strategies of the organization's future state.

strategy

Action plan to set the direction for the coordinated use of resources through programs, projects, policies, procedures, and organizational design and establishment of performance standards.

strengths-weaknesses-opportunities-threats (SWOT) analysis

Analysis used to determine where to apply special efforts to achieve desired outcomes. Entails listing (1) strengths and how best to take advantage of them; (2) weaknesses and how to minimize their impacts; (3) opportunities presented by the project and how best to take advantage of them; and (4) threats and how to deal with them.

strong matrix

Organizational structure in which the balance of power over resources shifts from the functional managers to the project manager, and the project manager has greater decision-making influence. *See also* weak matrix.

structured walk-through

Systematic, comprehensive review of the requirements, design, or implementation of a system by a group of qualified experts.

subcontract

Contract or contractual action entered into by a prime contractor or subcontractor to obtain supplies, materials, equipment, or services under a prime contract.

subcontracted items

Parts, components, assemblies, and services produced or performed by other than the prime contractor, according to the prime contractor's design, specifications, or directions, and applicable only to the prime contract.

subcontracting process

Process of acquiring personnel, goods, and services from external sources for new or existing work.

subcontractor
(1) Competent and qualified organization or person procured to perform work within specified elements of the project's WBS; serves as an adjunct member of the project team.
(2) Contractor, distributor, vendor, or firm that furnishes supplies or services to a prime contractor or another subcontractor.

subnet
Subdivision of a project network diagram generally representing some form of subproject. *Also called* subnetwork *or* fragnet.

subnetwork
See subnet.

suboptimization
Optimization of a subelement of a system, perhaps to the detriment of the overall system.

suboptimize
Do the best within one function or one area but with a potential cost to the larger whole.

subproject
Component of a project; often contracted out to an external enterprise or another functional unit in the performing organization.

substantial completion
(1) Point in time when the product is ready for use or is being used for the purpose intended and is so certified.
(2) Term used in construction contracting to mean substantial performance of contract requirements though not complete performance; often found when the contractor completes construction of the structure but fails to complete punch list items, install ornamental features, finish site cleanup, and so on.

subtask
Portion of a task or work element.

successor activity
Activity that starts after the start of a current activity.

summary level
Major subsystem level of a project WBS.

summary schedule
See milestone schedule.

summary work breakdown structure
Top three levels of a full WBS; these levels usually represent the formal cost and schedule reporting levels for a contract.

summative quality evaluation
Process of determining the lessons learned after the project is complete to document specific items that helped determine, maintain, or increase quality standards.

sunk costs
Costs that once expended can never be recovered or salvaged. Current thinking strongly suggests that sunk costs should not be considered a factor in deciding whether to terminate a project or allow it to continue to the next phase.

supplementary agreement
Contract modification accomplished by the mutual action of the parties involved.

supplementary conditions
Modifications, deletions, and additions to standard general conditions developed for particular goods or services.

supplementary information
Additional information collected from supplementary sources.

supplier
Person or organization responsible for the performance of a contract or subcontract.

supplier evaluation

Review and analysis of a response to a solicitation to determine the prospective supplier's ability to perform the work as requested. May include an evaluation of the prospective supplier's financial resources, ability to comply with technical criteria and delivery schedules, record of performance, and eligibility for award.

supplier ranking

Qualitative or quantitative determinations of prospective contractors' qualifications relative to the provision of the proposed goods or services.

supply chain integration

Synchronizing the efforts of all parties or stakeholders—suppliers, vendors, manufacturers, developers, dealers, distributors, and so on—to meet and exceed the needs and expectations of the customer, client, or end-user. With a focus on relationship-building, such integration results in strong bonds of trust and communication aimed at ensuring that the right products are delivered to the right places at the right time and at the right costs.

support staff

Individuals who provide assistance to the project team in areas such as financial tracking and project administration.

surety

Individual or organization that has agreed to be legally liable for the debt, default, or failure of a principal to satisfy a contractual obligation.

surgical team structure

Organizational structure in which a single individual has primary responsibility for the final product. Specialists produce pieces of the final output, which are given to the primary resource for integration into a completed product. Administrative and support personnel handle day-to-day administrative tasks, and the primary resource is backed up by an assistant who is available to take over in the event of the sudden loss of the primary. This approach can lead to consistent output in a relatively short time; however, friction can develop among the specialists and support staff, and the backup is seldom able to assume fully the primary's duties when called upon to do so.

SV

See schedule variance.

SWOT

See strengths-weaknesses-opportunities-threats analysis.

system

(1) Methodical assembly of actions or things forming a logical and connected scheme or unit.
(2) Set of functional capabilities rather than hardware.

system architecture

Manner in which hardware or software is structured, that is, how the system or program is constructed, how its components fit together, and what protocols and interfaces are used for communication and cooperation among the components, including human interaction.

system design

Translation of customer requirements into comprehensive, detailed functional, performance, or design specifications, which are then used to construct the specific solution.

system engineering

Logical sequence of activities and decisions to transform an operational need into a description of system performance parameters and a preferred system configuration.

system flowchart

See process flowchart.

system interfaces

Physical interfaces among connecting parts of a system, or performance interfaces among various functional or product subsystems.

system life
Period of time that begins when an information technology application is installed and ends when the users' need for it disappears.

systems approach
Wide-ranging, synthesizing method of addressing problems that considers multiple and interacting relationships. Commonly contrasted with the analytic approach.

systems thinking
Originated from a rigorous scientific discipline called General Systems Theory, which centers on the natural world and its living systems and governing laws. Emphasizes the value of viewing a system as a whole before examining its parts. By doing so, the environmental context of the system is better understood, resulting in greater appreciation and understanding of how the individual parts interact with the whole.

T

Taguchi method
Approach that uses statistical techniques to compute a "loss function" used to determine the cost of producing products that fail to achieve a target value.

tangible capital asset
Asset that has physical substance and more than minimal value and is expected to be held by an organization for continued use or possession beyond the current accounting period.

target completion date
See target date.

target cost
Negotiated amount of cost included in incentive contracts.

target date
(1) Date an activity is planned to start or end.

(2) Date generated by the initial CPM schedule operation and resource allocation process.

target fee
Amount the contractor will receive if its total allowable costs equal total target costs in a cost-plus-incentive fee contract.

target finish date (TF)
Date work is planned to finish on an activity.

target plan
Plan and schedule based on achieving the target date.

target profit
Amount of profit the contractor will receive if its total allowable costs equal total target costs in a fixed-price incentive contract.

target reporting
Reporting on the current schedule versus the established baseline schedule or "target" and the variance between them.

target start date (TS)
Date work is planned to start on an activity.

task
Well-defined component of project work; a discrete work item. There are usually multiple tasks for one activity. *See also* activity.

task definition
Unique description of each project work division.

task force
(1) Team of skilled contributors who are charged with investigating a problem for the specific purpose of developing and implementing a solution.
(2) Form of project organization usually used for small, uncomplicated projects.

task force organization
See projectized organization.

task type
Identification of a task by resource requirement, responsibility, discipline, jurisdiction, function, or any other characteristic used to categorize it.

task-oriented WBS
See work breakdown structure.

team
See project team.

team arrangement
Arrangement in which (1) two or more companies form a partnership or joint venture to act as a potential prime contractor or (2) a potential prime contractor agrees with one or more other companies to have them act as subcontractors.

team building
(1) Planned and deliberate process of encouraging effective working relationships while diminishing difficulties or roadblocks that interfere with the team's competence and resourcefulness.
(2) Process of influencing a group of diverse people, each with individualized goals, needs, and perspectives, to work together effectively for the good of the project.

team development
(1) Development of individual and group skills to improve project performance.
(2) Enhancement of stakeholders' ability to contribute as individuals and to function as a team.

team members
See project team.

team-building activities
Management and individual actions undertaken specifically and primarily to improve team performance.

teaming agreement
Agreement between two organizations to work together as partners in a venture, recognizing that each has specific skills that will contribute to an effective team relationship. The agreement lists their specific responsibilities and obligations and itemizes the distribution of revenues or other benefits resulting from the arrangement.

technical authority
See expert authority.

technical baseline
The project's work breakdown structure.

technical interfaces
Formal and informal working and reporting relationships among different technical disciplines involved in a project.

technical project leader
Person who serves primarily as the senior technical consultant on a team.

technical quality administration
Process in which a plan is prepared to monitor and control the technical aspects of the project so that they are completed satisfactorily. The plan also includes policies and procedures to prevent or correct deviations from quality specifications or requirements.

technical quality specification
Establishment and documentation of the specific project requirements, including execution criteria and technologies, project design, measurement specification, and material procurement and control, needed to satisfy the expectations of the client, stakeholders, and project team.

technical quality support
Provision of technical training and expertise from one or more support groups to a project in a timely manner.

technical requirements

Description of the features of the deliverable in detailed technical terms to provide project team members with crucial guidance on what needs to be done on the project.

technical specification

See specification.

technique

Skilled means to an end.

telecommuting

Performing one's job or project responsibilities at a location that is remote from one's office through the use of computers and telecommunications devices. Has become popular among organizations because it reduces the amount of time an employee spends traveling to and from the office, reduces pollution and traffic congestion, and generally improves employee morale and productivity.

templates

Set of guidelines that provides sample outlines, forms, checklists, and other documents.

temporary

Having a definite beginning and a definite end.

tender

(1) Solicitation of bids or proposals for goods or services. *See also* solicitation.
(2) Response to a solicitation submitted by a prospective contractor. *See also* offer.

term contract

In U.S. federal government procurement, a type of cost-plus-fixed fee contract in which the scope of work is described in general terms and the contractor's obligation is stated in terms of a specified level of effort for a stated period of time.

termination by addition

Ending the project by bringing it into the organization as a separate, ongoing entity.

termination by extinction

Ending all activity on the project without extending it in some way, such as by inclusion or integration.

termination by integration

Ending the project by bringing all its activities into the organization and distributing them among existing functions.

termination by murder

Ending the project suddenly and without warning, usually for a reason that is unrelated to the purpose of the project.

termination by starvation

Reducing the project's budget significantly so that progress stops without formally ending the project.

termination manager

Individual responsible for closing out the administrative details of a project.

terms and conditions

All the contract clauses.

test and evaluation

Process in which a system or selected components are compared with requirements and specifications through testing.

testing

Part of inspection that assesses the properties or elements, including functional operation of supplies or their components, by applying established scientific principles and procedures.

The 7 Wastes

Forms of waste that occur in a manufacturing plant and which have since been applied to other business environments. Developed by Toyota's former chief engineer Taiichi Ohno who asserted that the opposite of waste is value, and that the seven wastes are a set rather than individual entities. Also, they are productivity—not quality—related. They include the wastes of—

- Overproduction
- Waiting
- Transporting
- Inappropriate processing
- Unnecessary inventory
- Unnecessary motions
- Defects

Theory of Constraints (TOC)

Theory of continuous improvement of any system advanced by Eliyahu M. Goldratt. Requires recognition of the important role of the system's constraints, which are anything that limits the system from achieving higher performance. In project management, the constraint is the critical path. TOC breaks down the process into five steps as follows: identify the constraints, decide how to exploit the constraints, subordinate everything else to the exploitation decision, elevate the constraints, and finally, return to the previous steps if the constraint has been broken. Process helps managers identify what to change, what to change to, and finally, how to bring about the change to improve the system.

Theory W Management

Approach to software project management in which the project manager tries to make winners of each party involved in the software process. Its subsidiary principals are "plan the flight and fly the plan" and "identify and manage your risks." Suggested by Barry Boehem.

Theory X Management

Approach to managing people described by MacGregor. Based on the philosophy that people dislike work, will avoid it if they can, and are interested only in monetary gain from their labor. Accordingly, the Theory X manager will act in an authoritarian manner directing each activity of his or her staff.

Theory Y Management
Approach to managing people described by MacGregor. Based on the philosophy that people will work best when they are properly rewarded and motivated, and that work is as natural as play or rest. Accordingly, the Theory Y manager will act in a generally supportive and understanding manner, providing encouragement and psychic rewards to his or her staff.

Theory Z Management
Approach to managing people described by Arthur and Ouchi. Based on the philosophy that people need goals and objectives, motivation, standards, the right to make mistakes, and the right to participate in goal setting. More specifically, describes a Japanese system of management characterized by the employee's heavy involvement in management, which has been shown to result in higher productivity levels when compared to U.S. or western counterparts. Successful implementation requires a comprehensive system of organizational and sociological rewards. Its developers assert that it can be used in any situation with equal success. *Also called* participative management style.

Thomas-Kilmann Conflict Mode Instrument
Questionnaire used to measure how much competing, collaborating, compromising, avoiding, and accommodating behavior is displayed in conflict situations. Examines the extent to which individuals focus on assertive versus cooperative behavior in work situations.

three-point estimating
Technique that allows for uncertainty in estimates by defining the distribution of possible task durations according to three duration estimates: the minimum, the maximum, and the target.

threshold
Time, monetary unit, or resource level, placed on something, which is used as a guideline that, if exceeded, causes some type of management review to occur.

tied activity

Activity that must start within a specified time or immediately after its predecessor's completion.

tiger team

Group of objective specialists, convened by management, who evaluates, assesses, and makes recommendations for resolving problems associated with a particular area of concern.

tight matrix

Physical placement of project team members in one location.

tightened inspection

Inspection under a sampling plan using the same quality level as that of normal inspection but requiring more stringent acceptance criteria.

time value of money

Economic concept which purports that money available now is more valuable than the same amount of money at some point in the future due simply to its potential earning power, and not inflation as many believe. Used in calculating the present value of money for financial analysis as well as other purposes. *See* present value.

time variance

Scheduled time for the work completed less the actual time.

time-and-materials contract

Type of contract that provides for the acquisition of supplies or services on the basis of direct labor hours, at specified fixed hourly rates, for wages; overhead; general and administrative (G&A) expenses and profit; and materials at cost, including materials handling costs.

time-limited scheduling

Scheduling activities so that the limits on resource use are not exceeded, unless those limits would push the project beyond its scheduled finish date. Activities may not begin later than their late start date, even if resource limits are exceeded. Should not be used on networks with negative total float time.

time-scaled network diagram
Project network diagram drawn in such a way that the position and length of an activity represents its duration. Essentially, a bar chart that includes network logic.

TOC
See Theory of Constraints.

tolerance
(1) Specific range in which a result is considered to be acceptable.
(2) Range of values above and below the estimated project cost, schedule, or performance within which the final value is likely to fall.

tools and techniques
(1) Mechanisms applied to input for the purpose of creating output.
(2) Set of activities, services, instruments, or materials that enables the individual or project team to create, develop, and complete deliverables.

top-down budget
General, nondetailed projections often used to determine the range of possible costs for a project.

top-down estimating
Cost estimating that begins with the top level of the WBS and then works down to successively lower levels. *Also called* analogous estimating.

tort
Wrongful act that is neither a crime nor a breach of contract but renders the person committing the act liable to the victim for damages. An example would be a building owner's failure to repair a sidewalk causing a person to fall and break a leg. The law provides remedy for damages from the fall.

total allocated budget
Sum of all budgets allocated to the project, which consists of the performance measurement baseline including all reserves.

total certainty
Situation in which all information is available, and everything is known.

total cost
Sum of allowable direct and indirect costs that are allocable to the project and have been or will be incurred, less any allocable credits, plus any allocable costs of money.

total float
See float.

total quality management (TQM)
(1) Approach used to achieve continuous improvement in an organization's processes and products.
(2) Common approach to implementing a quality improvement program within an organization.
(3) Philosophy and set of guiding principles that encourage employees to focus their attention on ways of improving effectiveness and efficiency in the organization.

TQM
See total quality management.

traceability
(1) Ability to trace the history, application, or location of an item or activity by means of recorded identification.
(2) Ease with which a project can be traced forward from specifications to the final deliverable or backward from the deliverable to the original specifications in a systematic way.

trademark
Logo or insignia that differentiates one organization's goods from all others. Also, any mark, letter, design, picture, or combination thereof, in any form, that is used by a person to denominate goods that he makes; is affixed to the goods; and is neither a common nor generic name for the goods, nor a picture of them, nor merely a description of them.

trade-off

Giving up or accepting one advantage, or disadvantage, to gain another that has more value to the decision maker. For example, accepting the higher cost (a disadvantage) of a project because there will be more functionality (an advantage) in the delivered product.

training

Activities designed to increase the skills, knowledge, and capabilities of the project team.

transformational leadership

Motivational approach to management based on the philosophy and practice of encouraging employees to achieve greater performance through inspirational leadership. Such an approach is thought to develop employee self-confidence and result in higher achievement goals.

tree search

Evaluation of a number of alternatives that logically branch from each other like a tree with limbs.

trend analysis

(1) Use of mathematical techniques to forecast future outcomes based on historical results. Often used to monitor technical, cost, and schedule performance.
(2) Examination of project results over time to determine whether performance is improving or deteriorating.

trend report

Indicator of variations of project control parameters against planned objectives.

triple constraint

Term used to identify what is generally regarded as the three most important factors that a project manager needs to consider in any project: time, cost, and scope (specifications). Typically represented as a triangle, each of these constraints, when changed, will impact one or both of the others. They do not exist in isolation. For example, if the scope of a project increases, generally time and cost will also increase.

t-type matrix
Tool used to identify the root cause of problems resulting in design changes in new product development. Proper use of the matrix helps in understanding why the problem occurred and resulted in a design change; why the problem was not detected when it occurred; and how the design process can be improved so that similar problems can be eliminated or reduced in the future.

U

UCC
See uniform commercial code.

unacceptable risk
Exposure to risks that are significant enough to jeopardize an organization's strategy, present dangers to human lives, or represent a significant financial exposure, such that avoidance or mitigation is imperative.

unallowable cost
Cost incurred by a contractor that is not chargeable to the project on which the contractor is working.

uncertainty
(1) Situation in which only part of the information needed for decision making is available.
(2) Lack of knowledge of future events.

uncertainty allowance
Allocation of time or money to cover potential occurrence of risk events. *See also* contingency reserve *and* management reserve.

undistributed budget
Budget applicable to contract effort that has not been identified to CWBS elements at or below the lowest level of reporting.

uniform commercial code (UCC)

Code of U.S. laws governing various commercial transactions including the sale of goods, banking transactions, and other matters. Developed to bring uniformity to the laws of the various states. Has been adopted, with some modifications, in all states except for Louisiana as well as the District of Columbia and the Virgin Islands.

unit of product

Item inspected to determine whether it is defective or nondefective or to count the number of defects. May be a single article, a pair, a set, a length, an area, an operation, a volume, a component of an end product, or the end product itself. May or may not be the same as the unit of purchase, supply, production, or shipment.

unit price contract

Contract in which the contractor is paid per unit of service and the total contract value is a function of the quantities needed to complete the work.

unmanageable risk

Risk for which it is impossible to reduce the likelihood of occurrence or amount at stake.

unpriced changes

Authorized changes to a contract, the cost of which is negotiated during execution.

unsolicited proposal

Written proposal submitted on the initiative of the prospective contractor for the purpose of obtaining a contract not in response to a formal or informal request.

update

Revision reflecting the most current information on the project.

useful life

Amount of time during which a product will provide a return or value to its owner or user.

user
Ultimate customer for the product; the people who will actually use it.

user friendliness
Ease of learning or using a computer, software package, or system.

user requirements
Specific product, service, or other business need that the project is intended to meet.

utility theory
Theoretical approach to measuring a person's willingness to take a risk in light of the different levels of reward, whether that reward be for the person taking the risk or for other potential beneficiaries.

V

validation
Evaluation of a product against its specified requirements.

value analysis
Activity concerned with optimizing cost performance. Systematic use of techniques to identify the required functions of an item, establish values for those functions, and provide the functions at the lowest overall cost without loss of performance.

value chain
Series of interconnected, value-added activities, the sum total of which connect an organization's supply side with its demand side. Identifying and forging mutually-beneficial relationships with all the stakeholders in the value chain enhances an organization's ability to produce a product for, or deliver a service to, its customers at the highest level of quality at competitive prices. *See also* supply chain integration.

value engineering
Approach that examines each element of a product or system to determine whether there is a more effective and less expensive way to achieve the same function.

variable cost
Unit of cost that varies with production quantity, such as material or direct labor required to complete a product or project.

variables sampling
Sampling method in which the result is rated on a continuous scale that measures the degree of conformity.

variance
Actual or potential deviation from an intended or budgeted amount or plan. Difference between a plan and actual time, cost, or performance.

variance analysis
Comparison of actual project results to planned or expected results.

variance at completion (VAC)
In the earned value method, the difference between the BAC and the EAC (VAC = BAC – EAC).

variance report
Documentation of project performance related to a planned or measured performance parameter.

variance threshold
Predetermined cost, schedule, or performance parameter that, when realized, causes an action. For example, the project's cost-schedule variance threshold may be set at 20 percent, so that any variance greater than 20 percent would require an action, such as reporting the event to senior management, holding a project review, or redefining the project's scope.

variation

(1) Change to a contractor's work order under the terms of the contract.
(2) Degree of change or divergence among the members of a set or group.

vendor

Distributors of commonly available goods or services when requirements and specifications are well defined.

vendors conference

See bidders conference.

verification

Evaluation of the correctness of the output of various stages of the process based on the criteria for that stage.

verification, validation, and test (VV&T)

Process used to prove that a solution meets both specification and user requirements as evidenced by test and operational results.

version

Instance of a commercial or customized software application that reflects major changes in functions.

virtual team

Project team that is not physically colocated and whose interaction occurs primarily through electronic networks such as the internet, intranet, or other configurations to ensure a team environment is established and maintained.

vision

Basic theme or shared value that is important and meaningful to the members of the organization.

W

waiver

Intentional or voluntary relinquishment of a known right or
conduct that warrants an inference that the right has been
relinquished. Under the doctrine of waiver, a party can
relinquish rights he or she has under the contract. For example,
the right to strict performance is waived if the contractor
delivers incomplete or defective products or delivers after the
scheduled date and the project manager does not object or
demand that the defects be corrected.

walk-through

(1) A peer review and examination of the requirements, design,
or implementation of a project by qualified experts to ensure
that the project objectives will be met.
(2) Process used by software developers whereby a group of
knowledgeable peers mentally step through the design and
logic flow of a program with test cases to identify errors and
inconsistencies.
(3) Rehearsal of an operational procedure by simulating the
execution of all its steps except those that are high risk or
prohibitively expensive.

war room

Command and control center for a specific project, which also
serves as a conference area for the project client, senior
management, and other project stakeholders. Has the added
benefit of providing unmistakable identity to the project whose
team members may not work in close physical proximity.

warranty

Promise or affirmation made by a contractor regarding the
nature, usefulness, or condition of the supplies or services to be
furnished under the contract, based on one party's assurance to
the other that the goods will meet certain standards of quality
including condition, reliability, description, function, or
performance. Purpose is to establish a level of quality and to

give a source of remedy for loss because of a defect in the quality of goods.

warranty clause
Specific clause in a contract to provide the buyer with additional time after delivery to correct defects or make some other type of adjustment.

warranty of merchantability
Promise that goods are reasonably fit for the purpose for which they are sold and represented by the seller.

WBS
See work breakdown structure.

WBS dictionary
Collection of work package descriptions that includes, among other things, planning information such as schedule dates, cost budgets, and staff assignments.

WBS index
List of WBS elements set up by indenture.

weak matrix
Organizational structure in which the balance of power over project resources shifts in the direction of the functional manager, and the project manager has less decision-making influence and authority. *See also* strong matrix.

weighting system
Method for quantifying qualitative data to minimize the effect of personal prejudice. Used in project or contractor selection.

what-if analysis
Process of evaluating alternative strategies, by changing certain variables and assumptions to predict the outcome of considering such changes.

white paper
Narrative exposition on any topic advancing the thoughts and opinions of the author, the purpose of which may be to test the

author's idea by the readership, criticize a course of action proposed by the author's company or government, or advance a particular position. Often, but not necessarily, written and distributed anonymously. In the U.S. government, a white paper indicates the official government position on a particular public issue.

win-lose
Outcome of conflict resolution that typically makes use of the power available to each party and treats conflict as a zero-sum game.

win-win
Outcome of conflict resolution that results in both parties being better off. Focuses on the objectives of both parties and the ways to meet those objectives while resolving the issue at hand.

withdrawing
See conflict resolution.

withholding
Nonpayment of contract amounts by the buyer because the contractor failed to carry out some obligation under the contract.

work acceptance
Work is considered accepted when it is conducted, documented, and verified according to acceptance criteria provided in the technical specifications and contract documents.

work authorization
Permission for specific work to be performed during a specific period; generally used in cases where work is to be performed in segments because of technical or funding limitations. *Also called* work release.

work authorization system
Formal procedure for sanctioning project work to ensure that it is done at the right time and in the proper sequence.

work breakdown structure (WBS)

A hierarchically-structured grouping of project elements that organizes and defines the total scope of the project. Each descending level is an increasingly detailed definition of a project component. Project components may be products (a product-oriented WBS) or tasks (a task-oriented WBS). *See also* contract work breakdown structure.

work element

See task.

work item

See task.

work package

Deliverable at the lowest level of the WBS. May be divided into activities and used to identify and control work flows in the organization.

work package budget

Resources that are formally assigned by the responsible performing organization to accomplish a work package, expressed in monetary units, hours, standards, or other definitive units.

work release

See work authorization.

work results

Outcome of activities performed to accomplish the project.

work statement

See statement of work.

work unit

Calendar time unit when work may be performed on an activity.

workaround

Unplanned response to a negative risk event. Distinguished from contingency plan because it is not planned in advance of the occurrence of the risk event.

working calendar

(1) Calendar dates that cover all project activities, from start to finish.

(2) Calendar that reflects project work and nonwork dates (for example, holidays or planned shutdowns) and is used as a basis for network and schedule calculations in project management software.

working time

Period of time in which actual work on a project can be, and should be, completed. Working time will vary from project to project depending on its unique requirements. For example, replacing a large private branch exchange computer in an office building is commonly done on weekend days when most people are not in the office.

workload

Sum total of work that a person, group, or organization is responsible for completing within a given time period. May be expressed qualitatively, which is often a perception of the load based on the ability of a specific person to do it, or, quantitatively, which is usually based on historical data and experience.

workweek

Normal number of days or hours that is designated as that period of time in which project work will be conducted. Many organizations use 8 hours a day, 5 days a week as a standard workweek. However, this is adjusted based on workplace rules and regulations, culture, working conditions, site location, and any other variable that necessitates a change to the norm. Project managers must base their cost and schedule estimates on the workweek applicable to their project.

Z

ZD

See zero defect.

zero defect (ZD)

Quality standard, first articulated by Philip Crosby, that asserts that nothing less than 100 percent quality should be the goal of an organization.

zero variance

Situation in which the planned date or cost is equal to the actual date or cost of an activity or project. This is a rare event in most projects.

zero-based budgeting

Budgeting method, used in the 1970s, that was devised as an alternative to the incremental approach and in which the project budget was totally justified at every budget cycle.

zero–one-hundred approach

Method used to determine earned value applied to work packages that start and are expected to be completed within a month. No value is earned when the activity starts, but when it is completed 100 percent of the value is earned.

zero-sum game

Game in which the sum of the amounts won and lost by all parties is zero. Whatever is gained in such a game is always achieved at the expense of the other party. Many view implementing project management in an organization as a zero-sum game whereby project managers win power and authority at the expense of functional or line managers.

A Note to Our Readers

If you discover that we have missed a term that you think should be included in the next edition, please take a moment to let us know. We will be much indebted to you for your effort in helping us keep this glossary current, accurate, and complete.

Send us the term or phrase—and your interpretation of it—and we will present it to our Technical Advisory Board for inclusion in the third edition. Note that ESI will edit all submissions for clarity and style and retain the copyright on the final printed definitions.

Send your entries or other comments to—

Dixie Richards, Senior Editor
ESI International
4301 N. Fairfax Drive, Suite 800
Arlington, VA 22203

Fax: 1-703-558-4415
E-mail: drichards@esi-intl.com

More from ESI International

PMP Challenge!, J. LeRoy Ward and Ginger Levin, D.P.A. 1998. 540 pages. Spiral-bound. Second Edition. $44.95.

Quiz yourself on your knowledge of the PMBOK®, specifically, and project management, in general, with this flash card study aid containing 540 thought-provoking questions. This publication addresses the topics you need to know to pass the PMP® certification exam and will improve your chances of passing it the first time around.

PMP Exam: Practice Test and Study Guide, Editor, J. LeRoy Ward. 1998. 218 pages. Spiral-bound. Second Edition. $29.95.

Are you looking for a practice test that will provide an excellent representation of the types of questions you are sure to find on the PMP® certification exam? This publication contains 320 multiple-choice questions (40 per PMBOK® area)—including questions on the new project integration management area—and provides a rationale and a reference with each correct answer.

Risk Management: Concepts and Guidance, Editor, Carl L. Pritchard. 1997. 218 pages. Hardcover. $59.95.

Focusing on a systematic approach to risk management, this authoritative text includes more than a dozen chapters highlighting specific techniques to enhance organizational risk identification, assessment, and management, all within the project and program environments. The appendixes are rich with insight on applying probability, statistics, and other complex tools.

Nuts & Bolts #1: How to Build a Work Breakdown Structure, Carl L. Pritchard, 1999. 56 pages. Softcover. $25.00.

Although project managers are consistently expected to create the WBS as the cornerstone of their project plans, limited references are available on how to build one that works. This book describes several approaches to WBS construction, highlights the advantages and disadvantages of each, and examines the implications of their use.

246

Nuts and Bolts #3: Precedence Diagramming—Successful Scheduling in a Team Environment, Carl L. Pritchard, 1999. 62 pages. Soft cover. $25.00.

The biggest challenge in project management is bringing order to the sheer volume of competing priorities. By using precedence diagrams, project managers can clearly identify the sequence and interdependence of critical activities, clarify work processes, and solidify team member roles and buy-in. This concise overview teaches you how to construct and interpret precedence diagrams—the most common model used in software programs—and apply them to strengthen team commitment and project success.

To order one of the books, call 1-703-558-3020 or visit our Web site at http://www.esi-intl.com.

PM Appraise™: A Knowledge & Skills Assessment, ESI International, 1999.

A flexible, reliable tool for evaluating project management capabilities. Used to identify knowledge and skill in individual project managers as well as groups, in the experienced as well as novices. Its expanded and extensively revised content, corresponds to the Project Management Body of Knowledge (PMBOK®), as defined by the Project Management Institute. Individuals answer multiple-choice questions to determine the areas in which they require the most improvement. Organizations often use the composite results from groups to determine their educational and training priorities.

To find out more about this instrument, call 1-703-558-3020.

References

Adams, John R., and Bryan W. Campbell. *Roles and Responsibilities of the Project Manager.* Upper Darby, Pa.: Project Management Institute, 1990.

Bicheno, John. *The Quality 50: A Guide to Gurus, Tools, Wastes, Techniques, and Systems.* Melbourne Victoria, Australia: Nestadt Consulting Pty. Ltd., 1994.

Cable, Dwayne, and John R. Adams. *Organizing for Project Management.* Upper Darby, Pa.: Project Management Institute, 1982.

Carter, Bruce, Tony Hancock, Jean-Marc Morin, and Ned Robins. *Introducing RISKMAN Methodology: The European Project Risk Management Methodology.* Oxford, England: NCC Blackwell, 1994.

Cavendish, Penny, and Martin D. Martin. *Negotiating and Contracting for Project Management.* Upper Darby, Pa.: Project Management Institute, 1987.

Cleland, David I. Project Management: Strategic Design and Implementation. 2d ed. New York: McGraw-Hill, 1994.

U.S. Department of Defense. *The Program Manager's Guide to Software Acquisition Best Practices.* Washington, D.C.: U.S. Department of Defense, April 1997.

Fleming, Quentin W. Cost/Schedule Control Systems Criteria: The Management Guide to C/SCSC. Chicago: Probus Publishing, 1988.

Fleming, Quentin W. *Put Earned Value (C/SCSC) into Your Management Control System.* Worthington, Ohio: Publishing Horizons, 1983.

Frame, J. Davidson. Managing Projects in Organizations: How to Make the Best Use of Time, Techniques, and People. Rev. ed. San Francisco: Jossey-Bass, 1995.

Frame, J. Davidson. The New Project Management: Tools for an Age of Rapid Change, Corporate Reengineering, and Other Business Realities. San Francisco: Jossey-Bass, 1994.

Garrett, Gregory A. *World-Class Contracting.* Arlington, Va.: ESI International, 1997.

General Accounting Office. "Terms Related to Privatization Activities and Processes." GAO/GGD-97-121, July, 1997.

Ireland, Lewis R. *Quality Management for Projects and Programs.* Upper Darby, Pa.: Project Management Institute, 1991.

Kirchof, Nicki S., and John R. Adams. *Conflict Management for Project Managers.* Upper Darby, Pa.: Project Management Institute, 1989.

Lewis, James P. *Project Planning, Scheduling, and Control.* Chicago: Probus Publishing, 1991.

Mansir, Brian E., and Nicholas R. Schacht. *An Introduction to the Continuous Improvement Process: Principles and Practices.* Bethesda, Md.: Logistics Management Institute, 1988.

Martin, Martin D., C. Claude Teagarden, and Charles F. Lambreth. *Contract Administration for the Project Manager.* Upper Darby, Pa.: Project Management Institute, 1990.

Meredith, Jack R., and Samuel J. Mantel, Jr. *Project Management: A Managerial Approach.* 3d ed. New York: John Wiley and Sons, 1995.

Nash, Ralph C., Jr., and Steven L. Schooner. *The Government Contracts Reference Book: A Comprehensive Guide to the Language of Procurement.* Washington, D.C.: The George Washington University, 1992.

Project Management Institute Standards Committee. *A Guide to the Project Management Body of Knowledge.* Upper Darby, Pa.: Project Management Institute, 1996.

Rigby, Darrell K. *Management Tools and Techniques: An Executive's Guide 2000.* Boston, Ma.: Bain & Company, Inc., 1999.

Schmauch, Charles H. *ISO 9000 for Software Developers*. Milwaukee: ASQC Quality Press, 1994.

Soin, Sarv Singh. Total Quality Control Essentials, Key Elements, Methodologies, and Managing for Success. New York: McGraw-Hill, 1992.

Stuckenbruck, Linn C., ed. The Implementation of Project Management: The Professional's Handbook. Reading, Mass.: Addison-Wesley, 1981.

Stuckenbruck, Linn C., and David Marshall. *Team Building for Project Managers*. Upper Darby, Pa.: Project Management Institute, 1990.

Wideman, R. Max, ed. *Project and Program Risk Management: A Guide to Managing Project Risks and Opportunities*. Preliminary ed. Upper Darby, Pa.: Project Management Institute, 1992.